JOHN RYLANDS OF
MANCHESTER

D.A. Farnie

Published by the John Rylands
University Library of Manchester
Oxford Rd, Manchester, 1993

ISBN 0 86373 116 3

Figure 1: John Rylands in 1869
'Not slothful in business; fervent in spirit; serving the Lord'.
(Rom., 12: 11)

JOHN RYLANDS OF MANCHESTER

D.A. FARNIE★
DEPARTMENT OF HISTORY, UNIVERSITY OF MANCHESTER

★ I have been greatly helped by the comments of Dr J.C.G. Binfield, Mr Harold Smith and Mr Nicolas Barker, to whom I also remain indebted for his earlier comments upon the article on Mrs Rylands cited on p.101. I am also grateful to Mr Harry Horton and to Mr David W. Riley for suggesting several improvements in an early analysis of the Longford Hall Library Catalogue. Miss Glenise A. Matheson has saved me from certain errors of interpretation: those that remain are my own. Both Dr Clayton and myself are greatly indebted to Mr John Woodhouse, the head of the Library's Department of Conservation, for his services in enabling the illustrations to be reproduced in the most perfect form. The place of publication of works cited in the notes and bibliography is London, except where otherwise stated.

It is far more than a memory and a name that JOHN RYLANDS has bequeathed to this great commercial community; his career will long remain an inspiration and a power.

The Reverend Samuel G. Green in his funeral address, delivered on 15 December, 1888, and quoted in *In memoriam John Rylands born February 7 1801, died December 11 1888* (Chilworth: Unwin, 1889), 45.

1. *The significance of the career of John Rylands*

No other centre of business activity exerted such a hypnotic fascination upon the mind of Victorian England as did Manchester, 'the Chicago of the nineteenth century'.[1] No other industry so impressed the imagination of the world as did the Lancashire cotton industry. That industry transformed Manchester into a great city and made it the hub of a whole system of cities as well as the heart of a world-wide network of commerce. Thus by 1860 'Cottonopolis' had become a city of a hundred mills and a market for the products of another two thousand mills. That achievement was both unexpected and instructive. Manchester had few advantages to facilitate the growth of its commerce: it was neither born great nor did it have greatness thrust upon it. Rather did it achieve its metropolitan status through its own efforts and by the sheer force of its innate energies and resources.[2] Those energies were canalized through and harnessed by individual merchants and manufacturers pursuing their own interest but in so doing creating a wholly new way of life. Each new era of economic development seems to have been characterized by the rise of 'new men', courageous and enterprising, who boldly permit themselves to be driven by the wind actually blowing and who know how to trim their sails to take advantage of it.[3] Such new men became the most typical product of Victorian Manchester, a city which was both the cradle and the creation of 'the Manchester man'. Those men were dedicated to the service of the country's most important trade. They became apostles of the creed of individualism but they neither sought nor acquired publicity for themselves as individuals.

One of the most self-effacing of Manchester men excelled all others in the magnitude of his achievements. Those achievements need neither be exaggerated nor minimized. John Rylands may not be compared with Richard Arkwright as a supreme innovator responsible for ushering in a new industrial era. Nor did his firm serve as a 'national champion' since its greatest achievements were made in the home trade rather than in the world market. John

---

[1] L. Esher, *A broken wave: the rebuilding of England, 1940–1980* (Allen Lane, 1981), 274.

[2] R. Spencer, *A survey of the history, commerce and manufactures of Lancashire* (Biographical Publishing Company, 1897), 47.

[3] H. Pirenne, 'The stages in the social history of capitalism', *American Historical Review*, 19 (1914), 494–515.

Rylands differed from Arkwright in one fundamental respect, in his emphatic dissent from the established Church of England. His career reflects those links between Dissent and business success which Max Weber analysed in 1904. He did however strive for the reunion of the warring sects of the Church Universal some sixty years before the birth of the ecumenical movement proper. He remained essentially a-political in outlook, had nothing but scorn for officialdom and played no part in the political life of Victorian England. As a staunch Liberal he regarded Cobden and Bright as his heroes but he did not follow their example in forsaking trade for politics. His own career furnishes a striking contrast to that of Cobden, who never fulfilled the high hopes entertained in 1846 of his future career. Cobden's life in fact proved to be a series of unsuccessful speculations and left behind no continuing business-concern as a memorial. John Rylands devoted his great powers to private rather than to public ends and achieved within his chosen field a success without parallel.

Emerging from the humblest branch of manufacture, he built up by the 1860s the largest of firms within an industry which remained based primarily upon the small concern. He established branches in London and in Liverpool as well as in Manchester and finally extended his activity into the export market, so creating one of Lancashire's earliest multi-national enterprises. John Rylands became not only the leading merchant of a city noted for its merchant princes but also Manchester's first multi-millionaire. During the last thirty years of his life he successfully governed a vast integrated industrial and commercial empire. He established its foundations so securely that it survived his decease for over three score years. Like other Manchester merchants he was a Mancunian by adoption rather than by birth: unlike them, he remained loyal to the city of his adoption after he had become its leading merchant and had acquired an immense fortune. It was from a local journalist that he earned a panegyric.

Never since the days when Carthage and Venice were rendered so illustrious by the spirit of Commerce, and governed by oligarchies of royal merchants, has a more signal example of what can be achieved by the untiring industry and commercial aptitude of one man been apparent than in the case of JOHN RYLANDS, who is head of, perhaps, the largest and most important manufacturing and mercantile undertaking in the whole world.[4]

He undoubtedly left a profound impression upon the life of his generation. No other businessman approaches so closely to the ideal type of self-made man nurtured by 'Cottonopolis' during its greatest age. No other firm in the cotton industry was so much the lengthened shadow of one man as was that of Rylands & Sons.

[4] *Momus* (Manchester), 15 May 1879, 81, 'Our album. John Rylands Esq.'.

The words of Thomas Southcliffe Ashton (1889–1968), the most eminent historian of the Industrial Revolution, remain as true today as when they were first penned sixty years ago. 'The authoritative history of the Manchester merchant has yet to be compiled. When it is the name of Rylands will appear large on its pages'.[5]

Unlike the spokesmen of the Manchester school of political economy, John Rylands has earned no mention in the histories of Victorian England or even in the standard histories of the cotton trade. The reasons for that omission must remain a matter for speculation. One reason may be that he was a latecomer, reaching maturity in business after the classic period of the Industrial Revolution. Another may be that his greatest achievements were made within the humdrum sphere of the domestic market rather than of the exotic export trade. Undoubtedly he achieved his greatest measure of fame only posthumously when his widow decided to associate his name for ever with the accumulated wisdom of the ages. A study of this little-known career may serve two purposes. First, it will illuminate the history of the cotton industry over the long period extending from the age of the hand-loom to that of the industrial combine. Secondly, it will shed light upon a distinctive way of life which largely disappeared during the 1890s.

2. Rylands & Sons as a family partnership, 1819–42

The family of Rylands was native to Lancashire and to Cheshire, dating back apparently to the thirteenth century in Westhoughton and in Wilmslow.[6] The parents of John Rylands were Joseph Rylands (1767–1847) and Elizabeth Pilkington (1761–1829). The father was born in the village of Parr, near St Helens, which lay within the linen area of western Lancashire and within the economic orbit of Liverpool and Chester. The son of a yeoman and hand-loom manufacturer, he became in 1787 a manufacturer on his own account. His wife came from a more distinguished family than his own and bore him three sons and two daughters. Her nephew Richard Pilkington (1795–1869) became, in 1826, a glass manufacturer in St Helens. Her elder daughter married J.R. Cross and so established a link with another old Lancashire family. Elizabeth Rylands exerted a major influence upon her children and most of all upon her youngest son and most delicate child, John, who was born to her at the age of forty in 1801. Not only was he born at the very close of the 'extra-ordinary outburst of intellect'

    [5] T.S. Ashton, 'Rylands & Sons Ltd (1823): John Rylands merchant, industrialist and philanthropist', *Manchester Guardian Commercial*, 5 May 1934, 9.
    [6] J.P. Rylands, 'Rylands, of the Rylands, within Westhoughton, Co. Lancaster', *Genealogist*, 4 (1880), 170–8.

> *This place was erected*
>
> *in Memory of*
>
> *the late Mrs Rylands*
>
> *who departed this life*
>
> *the 9th May 1829*

Figure 2: Memorial to the Mother of John Rylands

In 1830 the Gidlow Lane Memorial School in Wigan was built in memory of Elizabeth Rylands (1764–1829), the eldest daughter of Richard Pilkington (1731–97) and the revered mother of John Rylands. In the north wall a tablet bore the inscription reproduced above. Beneath the floor of the north-east corner lay the Rylands Vault, containing the bodies of the four infant children of John and Dinah Rylands who died between 1830 and 1832.

The four were buried unbaptized and in unconsecrated ground because their father had in 1830 professed his exclusive faith in believers' baptism.

The school was closed in 1894 and demolished in 1898, the year before the John Rylands Library was inaugurated in Manchester.

which occurred in Britain during the second half of the eighteenth century, but he also conformed to the rule that persons of eminence were often very delicate infants.[7]

Like his father John Rylands first learned to weave and then, in 1817, became a hand-loom manufacturer and merchant on his own account, though on a very small scale. He also helped in the draper's shop, which his father had opened in St Helens in 1812, and there displayed a precocious shrewdness in mastering the skills of the retail trader. His aptitude for commerce became so apparent and so great that he was joined in 1818 by his two older brothers, Joseph and Richard. Together they embarked upon the wholesale trade, distributing goods to other drapers. Joseph controlled the business of manufacture while John served as a commercial traveller, toured Lancashire, Yorkshire, Cheshire, Shropshire and North Wales and marketed the firm's goods. In that field he proved so successful that the father joined his three sons in 1819 and merged his own considerable business with theirs in the new firm of Rylands & Sons. That concern undertook the hand-weaving of coloured and coarse linen and calico goods for the Chester trade. John Rylands speedily captured most of the trade of North Wales, benefiting from the high quality of his wares as well as from the Nonconformist revival within that region. His eldest brother removed northwards from St Helens to Wigan in 1820 and was followed first by John in 1821 and then by his father in 1824. Thus

[7] H. Ellis, *A study of British genius* (Constable, 1904, 1927), 11–12, 118–20.

Pedigree 1: The Rylands Family of St Helens and Manchester

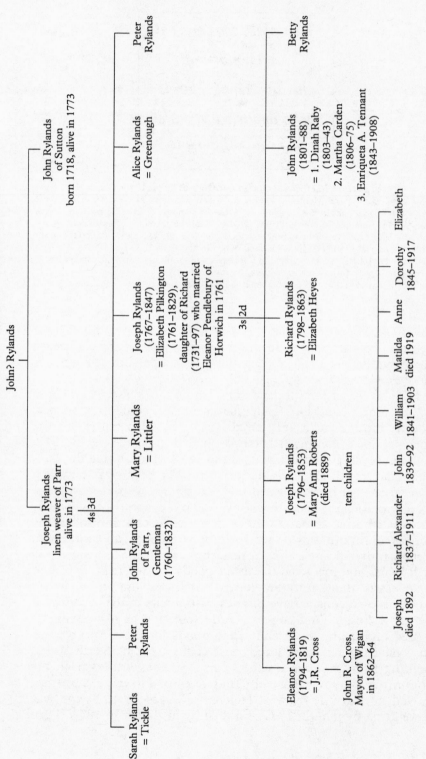

Source: Wills of John Rylands (d. 1832), Joseph Rylands (d. 1847), Joseph Rylands of Hull (d. 1853), Richard Rylands (d. 1863), J.G. Rylands (d. 1872), John Rylands (d. 1888), Mary Ann Rylands (d. 1889), Joseph Rylands (d. 1892), Enriqueta A. Rylands (d. 1908), and R.A. Rylands (d. 1911).

Pedigree 2: The Family of John Rylands

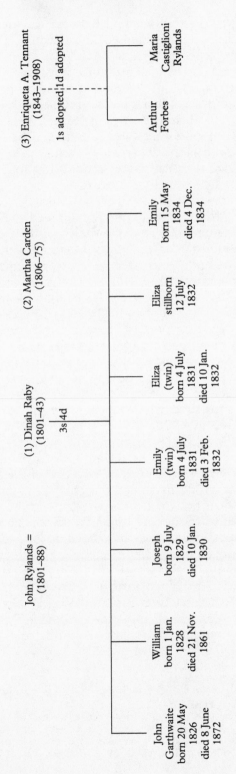

John Rylands = (1801–88)

(1) Dinah Raby (1801–43)

3s 4d

John Garthwaite born 20 May 1826 died 8 June 1872

William born 1 Jan. 1828 died 21 Nov. 1861

Joseph born 9 July 1829 died 10 Jan. 1830

Emily (twin) born 4 July 1831 died 3 Feb. 1832

Eliza (twin) born 4 July 1831 died 10 Jan. 1832

Eliza stillborn 12 July 1832

Emily born 15 May 1834 died 4 Dec. 1834

(2) Martha Carden (1806–75)

(3) Enriqueta A. Tennant (1843–1908)

1s adopted 1d adopted

Arthur Forbes

Maria Castiglioni Rylands

Source: Deeds of Joseph Rylands (1767–1847) in the Wigan Record Office, Leigh, D/DX/E1, Box 128/14, statutory declaration by John Rylands as to issue, 12 November 1855.

the firm abandoned a town which had become devoted to the chemical and coal industries, had acquired an unfavourably polluted atmosphere and lost its last cotton mill in 1842.[8]

The wholesale trade soon became more important than the retail trade as the main outlet for the products of the firm. In 1823 John Rylands ceased to act as a commercial traveller and opened a warehouse on behalf of the firm in New High Street, Manchester, a town which he had frequently visited in the course of business. He chose that market in a conscious departure from the tradition of the manufacturers of Wigan, who had hitherto produced solely for the Chester trade. He had however entered into competition as a country manufacturer with the established wholesale houses of Manchester, whose unfriendly reception encouraged him in self-defence further to challenge the existing customs of the trade. The entry into the Manchester market took place at the most opportune time for Rylands & Sons and contributed largely to the expansion of its activity, since the commerce of what Harrison Ainsworth was in 1851 to christen 'Cottonborough' grew faster than its manufacturing industry after the great mill-building boom of 1800–02. That growth harmonized with the postwar increase in numbers and wealth of the working-class markets of northern England and with the expansion of foreign markets. The population of the city increased by 45 per cent during the decade of the 1820s or faster than in any other decade of the century. Both economic and social life were stimulated by the successive foundation of the Manchester Chamber of Commerce in 1820, of the *Manchester Guardian* in 1821 and of the Royal Manchester Institution in 1823.

During the boom of 1822–25 Rylands & Sons extended operations from the sphere of manufacture into that of the finishing trades and became from 1824 dyers and bleachers on a small scale at Wigan. There the firm bought two large estates in the Douglas valley and in 1825 erected the Wigan Linen Works for the spinning of linen thread on throstle frames, so as to become independent of the market for its supply of yarn. The firm found, however, that the union of flax-dressers made the workmen 'independent, insolent and unreasonable'[9] and determined further to diversify its activity. In Manchester John Rylands defied local tradition by keeping his warehouse open to buyers during the midday 'dinner-hour' when other houses closed their doors. As the demand for the firm's

    [8] T.C. Barker and J.R. Harris, *A Merseyside town in the industrial revolution, St Helens 1750–1900* (Liverpool: University Press, 1954), 123.

    [9] Factories Inquiry Commission. Supplementary report of the central board of His Majesty's commissioners appointed to collect information in the manufacturing districts, as to the employment of children in factories, and as to the propriety and means of curtailing the hours of their labour (167 of 1834), part ii, vol. xx, 292–3, answers of manufacturers to queries: Joseph Rylands Jr, Wigan.

products outstripped supply, it began from 1829, at the instance of John Rylands, to sell other goods as well as its own products; it also became a merchant of goods for the Scotch and Irish markets. The sale of Scotch and Irish linen breached the monopoly hitherto held by the four or five Manchester linen houses and began the process of extending the firm's mercantile interests throughout the full range of manufactured textiles. During the 1830s the balance of its activities tilted decisively in favour of the cotton industry, especially after it acquired a cotton spinning mill in 1830. Linen became henceforward a luxury textile while cotton became the staple fabric of the new calico millenium which was about to dawn and which was so christened by Carlyle in 1850. That change of emphasis was faithfully reflected in the firm's entry in the Manchester directories. The 1832 directory described Rylands & Sons as 'linen and cotton spinners and manufacturers' but that for 1836 termed them 'cotton and linen spinners and manufacturers'. That shift in interest was fully vindicated when John Rylands observed, on a visit to Belgium, the distress amongst local linen weavers which was a direct result of the competition of the cotton textile industry. The Wigan estates increased in value after the construction in the 1830s of the North Union Railway linking Preston with the Liverpool–Manchester Railway at Parkside and converting the town into a major rail junction. The discovery on those estates of valuable coal seams enabled Rylands & Sons to become from 1839 colliery-masters as well as cotton spinners, so extending its interests into a field increasingly associated with the cotton industry.

The acquisition of a second manufacturing establishment brought the firm into the sphere of power-weaving, gave it mills in two separate centres and enabled John Rylands to develop a capacity for the delegation of authority to trustworthy managers. In 1839 he acquired a cotton mill at Ainsworth between Bolton and Bury and there began to produce 'domestics' (i.e. shirting and sheeting for the home trade) on power-looms for the Irish market, securing coal to raise the necessary steam power from a colliery rented from the earl of Wilton. That departure from the tradition of hand-loom manufacture took place in an old centre of hand-weaving but without apparent opposition since the firm fulfilled social functions by providing the village with a chapel, with schools and with a library. The entry into the sphere of a new technology seems to have been linked with an increase in the influence of John Rylands within the family partnership, whose bonds had begun to loosen after the death of the mother in 1829. John first took up residence in Manchester in 1834 and soon outstripped his elder brothers in the race for commercial success, so that he aspired to secure full freedom of action. Joseph, the eldest brother, retired from the firm and established in 1836 the Hull Flax and Cotton Mill Company, which became the first successful joint-stock company in the industry.[10] He managed that company until his death in 1853 when his son inherited his shares, his post and his aversion to trade unions. The father, Joseph Rylands senior, agreed in 1842 to dissolve the partnership. John Rylands preserved the original name of the firm but thenceforward became its supreme governor and remained its 'mainspring, prime mover and regulator'[11] during a period of sustained commercial expansion. By serving as his own partner, managing director and chairman he averted the unhappy consequences which might have ensued from any dissension or antagonism arising from the different personalities of the partners.

3. *John Rylands as an independent merchant, 1843–60*

Each new age brings forth new men and the cotton industry entered upon a new era after the acute depression of 1837–42. The average annual rate of expansion of the industry, as measured by its consumption of raw material, more than halved and sank from 7.4 per cent (1780–1840) to 3.3 per cent (1840–70).[12] It was however in this latter period that John Rylands expanded capacity most rapidly. That process began with the acquisition of the first mill which was truly his own and not part of the family business. In 1843 he secured his first mill in Manchester itself, so linking more closely the processes of manufacture with those of marketing. He leased Gorton Mills which had been built in 1825 by James Lillie, the engineer partner of William Fairbairn (Fig. 3). Their acquisition marked the beginning of 'a new era in my existence'.[13] The three mills had 26,264 spindles and 886 power looms with 121 cottages.[14] They were located on the bank of a branch of the Ashton Canal, which lead southwards to Reddish and Stockport, and the site adjoined the Manchester–Sheffield Railway. There he expanded the production of domestics on power looms and sought to provide for the social as well as the economic needs of his employees. He inherited a chapel and a Sunday School built by the Wesleyan Methodists. In 1845 he established at the mills a library of 600 volumes, a news-room and a school: the provision of such liberal facilities for the education of the workfolk earned the praise of a

[10] Joyce M. Bellamy, 'Cotton manufacture in Kingston upon Hull', *Business History*, 4 (1962), 91–100, 107–8. Joseph Rylands, *The distressed cotton operatives* (Hull: Goddard, 1864, 15pp.).

[11] *Manchester City News*, 15 April 1865, 3i, Reuben Spencer.

[12] D.A. Farnie, *The English cotton industry and the world market 1815–1896* (Oxford: Clarendon Press, 1979), 7.

[13] [S.G. Green], *In memoriam John Rylands* (Chilworth: Unwin, 1889), 55, quoting from the diary of John Rylands for 22 April 1843.

[14] *Catalogue of machinery, for preparing, spinning, winding, warping, dressing and weaving cotton goods. . . to be sold by auction by Mr Frost at the Gorton Works. . . 14th–25th June 1841* (Manchester: Richmond & Froggatt, 15th May 1841, 72pp.), in the Chapman Manuscripts.

Figure 3: Gorton Mills, c. 1842

These cotton mills were built by James Lillie in 1825 to the highest standards of the day and were largely fireproofed. The cost of construction was however very high, reputedly £120,000, and helped to bankrupt the first proprietor in 1840. John Rylands acquired them first on lease in 1842 and then by purchase, at a bargain price, in 1864. Their acquisition marked the beginning of his career as an independent business man because they were secured in his own name and not in that of the firm.

(Local Studies Library, Manchester Central Library)

Figure 4: Gidlow Mill, Wigan, in 1865

(Evan Leigh, The science of modern cotton spinning, 1873, 196)

Figure 5: Gidlow Mill in 1992

This detailed view of the mill's engine and boiler house is important for two reasons. First, it shows the skilful use of blue and white Staffordshire brick in order to create a harmony of colour. It explains why the Earl of Derby praised the whole structure as 'a new mill of vast extent . . . which is not, as usual, an eyesore but a pleasure to the eye to rest on, so well has architectural effect been studied in its construction' (*Manchester City News*, 15 April 1865, 3i). Secondly, it clearly shows on the side of both ventilation shafts the ends of the massive iron cross-ties which were inserted during construction in order to guard against any recurrence of the threat of subsidence. The survival of the reinforced structure for 130 years bears impressive testimony to the capacity of local builders and engineers.

(J.G. Farnie Esq.)

Figure 6: Mule Room in Gidlow Mill in 1932

A unique view of female mule spinners at work within the mule-gate. Mule spinners had been the highest paid of all cotton operatives since the 1790s and formed a social élite in the mill towns of Lancashire. Those spinners were usually male but John Rylands preferred to employ women, whose wages were lower than their male counterparts. They wore shoes at work, unlike the men. They were strong enough to manage the mule's operations while their manual dexterity in piecing proved to be superior to that of men.

(JRL, Archives of Rylands & Sons Ltd, Advertising Brochure c. 1935)

leading inspector of factories.[15] He refused to follow the example of other employers in working short-time during the first three months of 1847.[16] During those hard times he opened a provision shop, from which the operatives were supplied at wholesale prices.[17] He won the golden opinions of his weavers by strict compliance with the Ten Hours' Act of 1847 and earned their thanks in 1849 for not running his engines longer than ten hours per day. He invested in four collections of essays designed to serve as 'Working Men's Prizes'[18] and formed important plans for the future welfare of his workforce but was frustrated in their realization. He survived a two-months' strike against a reduction of 12 per cent in the wage-rates for weaving[19] and enlarged the opportunities for employment by building new weaving sheds in 1848 and 1854. In Gorton his firm created jobs mainly for women and girls while men worked in the railway workshops and in the locomotive-manufacturing firm of Beyer & Peacock established in 1854.

In the sphere of trade John Rylands began to extend the number of departments in the Manchester warehouse, where sixteen separate premises along the length of New High Street were converted into one large building. He established a fustian department in 1847 to handle the clothing most commonly worn by the labouring orders of society: he undertook the dyeing and finishing of all fustians sold by the firm and provided continuity of employment in a trade peculiarly liable to suffer from severe periodic depressions. In 1849 he opened a warehouse in London itself and so gained access to the greatest single market of the home trade. Under the influence of metropolitan demand he expanded the range of the firm's operations from the heavy textile trade in fustian, gingham, checks and linen into the prestigious and profitable fancy trade. As the linen industry began to adopt the power-loom and became increasingly centred in Ulster he withdrew from the Wigan Linen Works in 1854 and concentrated his manufacturing interests within the cotton industry. The resources of Rylands & Sons were great enough to enable it to survive a disastrous fire in 1854. That fire destroyed buildings and stock in New High Street worth over £200,000[20] but did not prevent the firm from reaping larger returns in 1854 than in 1853. By then John Rylands had become the largest textile merchant in Manchester[21] as

[15] *Reports of the inspectors of factories*, 31 Oct. 1846, 7, Leonard Horner, 2 Dec. 1846.

[16] J. Higson, *The Gorton historical recorder* (Droylsden: Higson, 1852), 147.

[17] Higson, 192, 196.

[18] First Prize, *Heaven's antidote to the curse of labour* (1849) by J.A. Quinton; Second Prize, *The light of the week* (1849) by John Younger; Third Prize, *The torch of time* (1849) by David Farquhar, *The pearl of days, or Advantages of the Sabbath to the working classes, by a labourer's daughter* [i.e. Barbara H. Farquhar] (1848).

[19] Higson, 204, 206, 208.

[20] *Manchester Guardian*, 4 March 1854, 7iv–vi, 8i–ii.

[21] D. Puseley, *The commercial companion* (Hall, 1858), 190.

well as a millionaire, being the first native of Lancashire to achieve that status. He had joined the Anti-Corn Law League in 1843 after a visit to Belgium, which had taught him the importance of labour-costs in the contest for the world market: on 3 August 1846 he stopped production at Gorton Mills in order to celebrate the repeal of the Corn Law.[22] He nevertheless rose to fortune on the basis of the home trade and not on that of the export trade, conducting business from his own warehouses rather than upon the floor of the Exchange. After the death of James Morrison of London (1789–1857) he became the leading textile merchant in the land.

4. The assumption of primacy within the cotton industry by the firm of Rylands & Spencer, 1861–72

The Cotton Famine of 1861–65 presented a major challenge to the industry by halving its supplies of raw material. That crisis encouraged many leading employers to withdraw from active business life. It also opened up new opportunities to such firms as those of Rylands & Sons, Tootal Broadhurst Lee & Co. of Bolton, Richard Haworth of Ordsall and Elkanah Armitage of Pendleton, all headed by Dissenting millowners. Those firms seemed to have drawn new strength from the celebration by Dissenting congregations of the bicentenary of the expulsions of 1662. The opportunities offered to such employers were generated by the extensive fluctuations in prices in association with two dominant trends, a huge inflation of prices between 1861 and 1864 and then a prolonged deflation from the peak level of prices registered in Liverpool on 25 July 1864,[23] lasting until 1869. Rylands & Sons were not one of the dozen firms, largely owned by Dissenting millowners, which continued to work their mills full-time throughout the Cotton Famine. From 1864, however, they undertook a marked expansion of their operations under the influence of John Rylands's new associate who filled in some measure the gap left in 1861 by the death of his son. Reuben Spencer (1830–1901) had first joined the firm in 1847. Being a member of a Congregational church and a Liberal like his employer, he rose to become 'his very confidential friend and manager – in short his *alter ego*'.[24] He became a partner in the firm in 1867 and sponsored the publication of its first history.[25] He supplied the main

---

[22] Higson, 195.

[23] *Manchester Guardian*, 26 July 1864, 4ii.

[24] *Manchester City News*, 1 April 1865, 2vii.

[25] R. Spencer, *History of Lancashire* (1897), 175–244; W.B. Tracy and W.T. Pike, *Manchester and Salford at the close of the nineteenth century: contemporary biographies* (Brighton: Pike, 1899), 131; H.H. Bassett (ed.), *Men of note in finance and commerce, with which is incorporated men of office. A biographical business directory 1900–1901* (Wilson, 1901), 202–3; *Manchester Guardian*, 23 May 1901, 5i, 7v; *Manchester City News*, 25 May 1901. The firm's history may be found in the *Manchester City News*, 1 April 1865, 2vi, 3i–ii; 8 April, 2v–vii, 3i; 15 April, 2v–vii, 3i–ii, 'Principal Manchester firms – their rise and progress. No. V. Messrs Rylands and Sons'.

driving force in the expansion of its operations. Three separate manufacturing establishments were purchased in Manchester. Those acquisitions restored the balance between the industrial and the commercial resources of the firm, its trade having expanded since 1843 far more rapidly than its own production. In 1864 Rylands bought the Irwell Works of the Manchester Wadding Company in Water Street together with the Medlock Mills in South Junction Street, Medlock, to the west of Oxford Street. He also bought the Dacca Mills of the Dacca Twist Company in Lower Mosley Street. At the Medlock Mills the firm undertook the large-scale manufacture of clothing, especially of shirts, on industrial sewing machines. That new venture expanded at the expense of its fustian trade but set an example which apparently proved too daring for any other firm in the cotton industry to follow since few possessed such secure commercial outlets. The Manchester Wadding Company turned cotton-waste into wadding which it dyed for use in the manufacture of clothing. The Dacca Mills produced a single class of goods in domestics but on a large scale. The enlarged Gorton mills with their 63,000 spindles, 1,500 looms, thirty acres and 150 appurtenant cottages were bought in 1864 when their twenty-one year lease expired: they were then extended by the addition of another large weaving shed and linked to the warehouse in New High Street by means of a private telegraph. The acquisition of those Manchester mills notably extended the range of the firm's operations in a vertical direction and gave it control over its sources of supply as well as over its markets. Those establishments formed a small empire unequalled in extent by any other local firm and were subject to as close and direct a superintendence as the warehouses themselves. They also gave to Rylands & Sons two new trading styles in the Dacca Mills Company and the Manchester Wadding Company, names which the firm carefully preserved. The warehouses had reached a height of seven storeys in 1862 and they extended by 1864 from one end of New High Street to the other: they had become the summit of the firm's hierarchical organization, the seat of its central power and the goal of all ambitious employees. Their stocks extended over the whole range of dry goods, including smallwares, haberdashery, clothing, millinery, furs and mantles, as well as all types of textiles. Rylands also re-equipped the Ainsworth mills, which had won a high reputation for their croydons. Above all, between 1863 and 1865 he built model mills at Wigan (Figs 4, 5 & 6). The partner of John Rylands in the new Gidlow Works was his nephew, John R. Cross of Gidlow House, who was the son of his sister Eleanor and who served as the mayor of Wigan in 1862–64 as well as a J.P.

Gidlow Mill remained unique amongst the seventeen mills operated by the firm as the sole purpose-built factory. John Rylands preferred to buy second-hand mills in good condition in order to secure the best possible value for money. Constructed after the death of his son and heir in 1861, the Gidlow Works was one of the finest cotton mills ever built and may have been designed to serve as a memorial to the proprietor. The mill cost over £100,000 at a time when building and machinery prices were depressed during the Cotton Famine. It provides the best contemporary example of what *The Times* of 13 April 1865 called 'the great manufactories occupying, one may say, the very front of English civilisation'. The proprietors, Rylands & Cross, had employed the leading mill architect of Lancashire, the Wesleyan Methodist George Woodhouse of Bolton (1829–83). Woodhouse was reputedly associated with the building of more mills than any other man in Lancashire. He was the architect of the Sunnyside Institute and Mills built by Tootal's in 1862–69 at Daubhill, Bolton, as well as the joint architect of Bolton Town Hall (1866–73). His Gidlow works established new standards in mill construction. Costs were raised by construction to the highest possible standard and by fireproofing the mill throughout. The number of storeys was restricted to three instead of the usual five. The nine turrets rising above roof level surmounted ventilation shafts. The chimney soared to a height of 204 feet in order to minimize any pollution of the atmosphere. With its own private spur railway as well as collieries, the mill held 60,000 spindles and 1,500 looms, extending the manufacturing power of the firm even more than its spinning power. It also introduced continuity into the technique of manufacture, whereby raw cotton was unloaded on the top floor and flowed downwards through successive labour-saving processes until it was finally woven into Dacca calico in the adjacent single-storeyed sheds shown in the foreground of Figure 4.

By 1865 the employees of Rylands & Sons numbered 4,500 (Table 1) or more than those employed by Horrockses of Preston or by any other concern in the cotton industry, while another 6,500 workpeople were engaged indirectly upon its orders. The basis of the firm's power remained unaltered in its control over the marketing of its products to the country's drapers. The number of its travellers had increased from four in 1840 to nineteen in 1865 and the number of its departments from four to thirty-three, while Henry Bannerman & Sons had twenty-one departments and J.P. & E. Westhead had fifteen departments. The number of hands employed in the Manchester warehouse had risen from twenty-eight to 600 while S. & J. Watts employed 200 and Westhead's employed 150. The number of its customers had increased five-fold to 10,000 in fifteen years. Its annual turnover may be presumed to have been of the order of some £1,500,000 since Westhead's enjoyed a turnover of £1,000,000 from some 7,000 accounts.

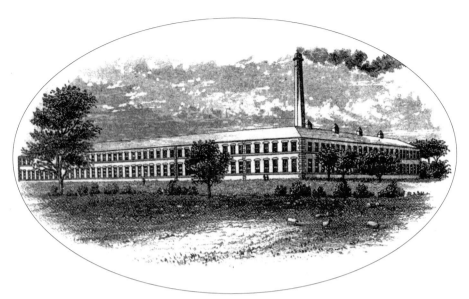

Heapey Bleach Mills

Dacca Mill

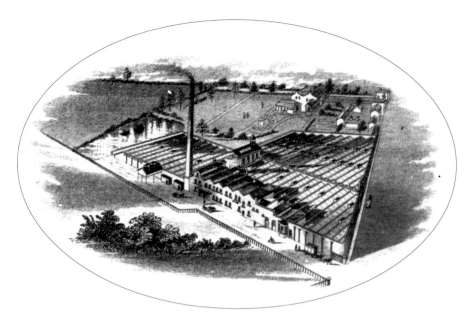

Swinton Mill

Figure 7: Heapey Works, Dacca Mill and Swinton Mill, *c.* 1885

Heapey Bleach works was leased in 1870 and purchased in 1895. It employed more steam power than any other of the firm's works, consuming 370 tons of coal weekly as well as four million gallons of water daily. As the home of the celebrated Heapey finish, it remained outside the Bleachers' Association formed in 1900. Its valuation was revised in 1915 from £150,435 to £116,000.

Dacca Mills on Water Street at the confluence of the Rivers Irwell and Medlock were acquired in 1865 under the name of the Irwell Works of the Manchester Wadding Co. They were renamed in 1873, leased in 1889 and sold in 1909.

Swinton Mill was built on Worsley Road in 1843 and was one of the earliest spinning mills in Swinton and Pendlebury; it was bought from John Bowers (1818–90) in 1874, together with 26 cottages, a beerhouse and a shop. It was renamed the Dacca Twist Mill and was demolished in 1983, the site being marked by Daccamills Drive.

(*JRL, Archives of Rylands & Sons Ltd, Register of Trade Marks, 1886*)

In 1866 John Rylands opened the firm's first branch in Liverpool. In 1870 he was forced to undertake a further measure of vertical integration by the self-defensive refusal of the bleachers to supply his firm. He leased the Heapey Bleach Works near Chorley (Fig. 7) and turned it into the largest bleaching and finishing works in Europe, employing the excellent local water and 600 hands in order to create what became renowned as the distinctive 'Heapey finish'. He raised the standard of production of bleached calico even more than that of unbleached, being an advocate of pure rather than of filled finishes, such as were produced by oversizing. That policy accorded with his belief in honesty and quality, with his dependence on the home trade rather than on the export market and with his pioneer use of the sewing-machine, whose needles tended to break when trying to pierce oversized cloth. Rylands also extended his manufacturing interests outside Lancashire into Yorkshire and Cheshire. The growing demand for Dacca and Longford sewing cottons led him in 1871 to lease a bobbin-mill at Helmsley[26] which however proved unprofitable and was abandoned before the expiry of the seven-year lease. In 1872 his partner Reuben Spencer bought the large Longford Buildings on Oxford Road in Manchester for the manufacture of clothing. In the same year Spencer also leased the Longford Works in Crewe[27] for the local manufacture of clothing on sewing-machines by women and girls, whose labour was cheaper than that available in Lancashire because of the lack of opportunities for female employment in a railway town. In 1873 John Rylands celebrated his commercial jubilee, having completed fifty years in trade in Manchester and achieved the great aims which he had set himself. His position had, however, become like that of Frankenstein since the partnership of Rylands & Spencer had almost passed beyond individual control and required some measure of reorganization before any new expansion might be undertaken.

5. The external interests of John Rylands and the creation of the library at Longford Hall, 1830–69

John Rylands was a cradle Congregationalist but his faith remained largely conventional until 1829 when the death of his mother caused him deep distress. He then adopted the views of the Baptists and, at the age of twenty-nine in 1830, he was baptized at the chapel of John Birt (1787–1862) in York Street, Manchester. He remained a member of that chapel until 1842 when Birt ceased to be pastor.[28]

---

[26] J. McDonnell (ed.), *A history of Helmsley, Rievaulx and district* (York: Stonegate Press, 1963), 167–8.

[27] W.H. Chaloner, *The social and economic development of Crewe, 1780–1923* (Manchester: University Press, 1950), 93, citing the *Crewe Guardian*, 16 Nov. 1872, 4vi; 25 Jan. 1902, 4vii and 1 Feb. 1902, 4iv–v.

[28] [S.G. Green], *In memoriam John Rylands* (1889), 16–17.

His marriage in 1825 to Dinah Raby had been celebrated at St John's Church in Manchester. Two sons were born, John Garthwaite in 1826 and William in 1828. Grave misfortune then overtook his newly-born children. During the five years 1829–34 five children were born and all five soon died: their average life-span was just over six months and the last four baby girls were not baptized. Those successive bereavements followed upon the loss of his beloved mother and led to his removal from Wigan, with its tragic domestic associations. In 1834 he took up residence in Manchester and also became a deacon of John Birt's chapel, the only ecclesiastical office he is known to have held during a long lifetime.

In Manchester John Rylands had seven successive residences before he finally settled in Stretford. For the first decade of his Manchester life he had taken lodgings at 7 Green Street, off Tib Street, close to the firm's warehouse. Later he lodged in Lever Street, with Charles Rowley. Only in 1834 did he acquire a country house on Smedley Lane in the northern suburb of Cheetham Hill. He also secured, by 1834, a town house at 3 Newton Street, near Hilton Street. Then in 1843 his wife died at the age of forty, leaving him with two sons. In 1844 he acquired Gorton Villa, a 'capital mansion house' built in 1829 and appurtenant to the mills. In 1848 he married the widow Martha Carden at St Peter's Church, Newton le Willows, to the southeast of St Helens. He had known Martha since their childhood together in Parr but no issue followed from the union. However within four months of the wedding he parted from his eldest son after concluding with him a formal agreement. John Garthwaite Rylands withdrew from the firm of Rylands & Sons and went to lead the life of a country gentleman at Orrell, near Wigan, and received from his father a regular remittance, which rose to £16 per month.[29] We cannot yet account for the rupture of the relationship between father and son. It may have stemmed either from the remarriage of the father or from the marriage of the son or from some other factor altogether. The result of the breach was to focus the father's hopes for the future upon the second son William.

The remarriage may also have affected the church membership of John Rylands. Since 1842 he had attached himself to the Congregational Church in Mosley Street, where Dr Robert Halley had been pastor since 1839. That church moved to a new site at Cavendish Street in 1848 and John Rylands made four separate contributions towards its building fund between 1845 and 1850. He did not, however, attend the church for three years after its migration. Only in 1851 was he formally received with his wife into

---

[29] John Rylands Library [hereafter cited as 'JRL.'], Archives of Rylands & Sons Ltd, Wages Ledger 1870–80, 45–60, private accounts.

membership. Martha Rylands proved even more regular in worship at Cavendish than her husband, averaging a 68 per cent attendance at the monthly communion service (1862–74) compared to the 62 per cent of her husband. John Rylands remained in communion with Cavendish longer than with any other church, leaving only in January 1876 after the death of Martha and his second remarriage.[30]

At Gorton he had encountered strong opposition to his efforts to improve the conditions of his employees. The prolonged strike of 1849 seems to have ended that particular phase of his social work. Together with his remarriage, it inspired his removal in 1850 from Gorton Villa to No. 24, Ardwick Green. Ardwick failed, however, to suit his convenience for very long, perhaps because of the industrial development to the east of the city. He decided to migrate westwards in search of fresh air and open space and he found new fields for social endeavour in Greenheys rather than in Gorton. In 1855 he bought the extensive Longford Hall estate in Stretford, where the home-trade merchants of Manchester had established their 'country residences'. There he made his home in 1857 in a new hall built in Italian style. He developed an immediate and keen interest in planning the landscape of the new estate. His guiding principles were the same ones which governed his business dealings, i.e. system, order and economy. Similarly within the firm he applied the techniques of the dedicated gardener, cultivating both customers and staff whilst weeding out the tares. At Longford Hall he paid special attention to irrigation and to horticulture. All the water draining off the roof was collected in a deep well and was then pumped up to a high-level tank. The meadows fronting the hall were irrigated by subterranean piping. Extensive gardens and conservatories were laid out on the pattern of Chatsworth. A large staff of nineteen gardeners was employed and special houses were built for them, Longford Cottages, to the rear of the hall. The kitchen garden was doubled in extent from two acres in 1862 to four in 1867. Fourteen conservatories with three-quarters of an acre under glass in 1862 were doubled in number to thirty one by 1875, with two miles of steam-pipes, serviced by six boilers, a steam engine and a gas-works. Exotic fruit such as grapes, peaches and pineapples were cultivated on a large scale, regularly carrying off prizes at exhibitions between 1874 and 1878.[31] Above all, he grew

[30] The membership rolls of Cavendish, listed at M162 in the Archives Department of the Manchester Central Library, do not include any entry for Miss E.A. Tennant, although the pastor Joseph Parker spoke of Mr Rylands, Mrs Rylands and Miss Tennant as 'names which always went together in the congregation connected with my ministry' (1858–69). Nor was Mrs Rylands a church member during Cavendish's jubilee year of 1898.

[31] *Journal of Horticulture and Cottage Gardener*, 47 (28 Jan. 1862), 353–4; 47 (18 Feb. 1862), 417–18, T. Appleby, 'Longford Hall'. *Gardener's Chronicle*, 16 Aug. 1875, 195–6; 21 Aug. 1875, 226–7, T. Baines, 'Longford Hall, Stretford'. Manchester Botanical & Horticultural Society, *Reports of the Council*, 1875–79. G.H. Pike, *Dr Parker and his friends* (Unwin, 1904), 51.

vegetables for sale, to the astonishment of the more traditionally minded.

The purchase of the Longford estate opened a new era in his existence. It was then that he began to assume posts of responsibility in the city and the county, serving in 1857 as high constable of Salford Hundred and as an hereditary governor of the Royal Manchester Institution. After the rupture with his eldest son he concentrated his hopes for the perpetuation of his name upon his second son, William Rylands (1828–61), whom he admitted to the business in 1852 and to partnership in 1859, so that the firm consisted of father and son.[32] In 1861 he was completely shattered by the death of his sole heir, which was followed in 1863 by the death of his last surviving brother.

Deep, poignant, and inconsolable was his father's grief. All his fond hopes respecting him were blighted, for he had reckoned on his being not only his own solace and stay in the evening of life, but that he would by his virtues, talents, and property be a great blessing in his lifetime, more especially to his native city, Manchester, and perpetuate the name of Rylands with honour to future generations.[33]

William's death left a void in his life and marked a fundamental turning point in his existence since it compelled him to modify drastically and irrevocably his deepest aspirations.

After the loss of his son John Rylands extended his activity in the field of social work, especially in the district of Greenheys where much of his time, effort and money was spent and where Martha vigorously supported him in the pursuit of their 'great hobbies'.[34] First, he became from 1855 a life member of the Manchester and Salford Asylum for Female Penitents, established in 1822 with John Birt as secretary; he also served as a house steward and from 1871 as treasurer, in succession to Elkanah Armitage. Secondly, in 1864 he established in Webster Street a female orphan asylum with accommodation for up to twenty girls. He soon moved it to larger premises at 14 Greenhill Street, next door to Greenheys Congregational Chapel, with accommodation for fifty girls. He himself served as the patron of the renamed Rylands Home and Orphanage and he secured two Lancashire M.P.s to serve as successive presidents in the persons of the merchant Benjamin Whitworth (1816–93) and the calico printer F.W. Grafton (1816–90). Thirdly, in 1865, he and Martha co-founded, together with Mr and Mrs William Woodward, a new institution in Burlington Street, the Servants' Home and Free Registry. That

[32] D. Puseley, *The commercial companion*, second edition (Hall, 1860), 154.
[33] *Manchester City News*, 15 April 1865, 2vi, reprinted in R. Spencer, *The home trade of Manchester* (Simpkin, 1890), 148.
[34] *Manchester City News*, 15 April 1865, 3ii.

organization provided respectable servants with temporary board and lodging and maintained a registry for the benefit of both servants and employers. Fourthly, he supported the successive establishment in 1870 of the Manchester & Salford Boys and Girls Refuges and Homes and in 1871 of the Manchester Religious Institute, for the joint use of three voluntary societies.[35]

The creation of his own library seems to have taken place during the period of William's last fatal illness. That library played an important role in his personal life. His formal education may have ended at the age of fifteen but he had been taught by his mother Elizabeth to revere literature. When the mother died the family decided to commemorate her not by means of a marble plaque but by the establishment of a school for the benefit of future generations. Elizabeth Rylands was duly commemorated by the foundation of Gidlow Lane School upon the family's Wigan estate. That precedent was in turn followed in 1889 when John Rylands's widow decided to honour his memory by founding a great library for the benefit of posterity. Elizabeth had inculcated in her son a profound belief in the value of education as the guide to conduct and as the guardian of liberty. Her influence ensured that her son continued to learn throughout his life and to help in the education of others. To that end John Rylands built up his own collection of books, a collection which was apparently dispersed some thirty years later.

The main evidence of the existence of the library at Longford Hall is supplied by a catalogue compiled during the Christmas season of 1881.[36] The work consists of two volumes, a reference catalogue and a numerical catalogue. The Reference Catalogue arranges the works in alphabetical sequence. It uses as key words author, title and subject (including places). Occasionally the date of publication is entered in red ink but for most of the works no such date is given. Hence where a book passed through more than one printing it may be difficult to specify which particular edition was held at Longford Hall. The Numerical Catalogue contains more concentrated and briefer entries than the Reference Catalogue, which has perhaps treble the number of entries in its 104 double pages. It allots a number to every book but uses only forty-three pages in order to list 1781 titles and includes two loose manuscript pages numbered 43(a) and 43(b). It also includes a prefatory

[35] W.B. Tracy and W.T. Pike, *Manchester and Salford at the close of the nineteenth century* (Brighton: Pike, 1899), 259. *Manchester Guardian,* 29 June 1871.

[36] JRL., English Manuscript No.1140. In the following paragraphs dates of a publication are given in two distinct forms. Those in roman type signify a date entered in the catalogue. Those in italic type have been derived from other sources and indicate the first recorded date of publication of a work. Where a book was not reprinted the italic date may reasonably be assumed to be the date of the work held at Longford Hall.

diagram showing the distribution of books among five bookcases. No entries at all are shown for the sixth bookcase and the final number for Case V (1336–1580) is written in pencil, presumably so that future additions might be made. It also includes notes pencilled in the right-hand margin by the side of many titles, relating to the manner of their disposal and including an occasional entry of 'Sale'.

Inevitably we remain profoundly ignorant about most aspects of the collection. We do not know whether John Rylands used advisers in the selection of books, or which booksellers secured his custom or whether they were based in Manchester or London. Nor do we know who compiled the catalogue or who borrowed those initial volumes of multi-volume sets which were recorded in 1881 as missing from the shelves. We can however be certain that the catalogue remained incomplete and never comprised a full tally of John Rylands's holdings. Indeed it does not seem to have been the first catalogue to have been compiled. Already by 1865 the Library at Longford Hall housed 'a large number of very valuable and carefully selected books classified in that very methodical manner which so characterises their owner'.[37] Such a classification would have been difficult without some form of catalogue. It even remains uncertain exactly where the library was housed: the hall had two 'bookrooms' in 1893 and at least nineteen bookcases in 1908,[38] including eight in the sanctum used by the owner for his biblical research, the Billiards Room. The 1881 Catalogue refers however to the contents of only five out of nineteen cases, leaving a very substantial number of books outside its purview.

John Rylands supplemented his own resources by making use of the other library to which he had access. Apparently he never joined any local literary society but he did buy a share in the Portico Library within two years of opening a Manchester warehouse and he retained it for twenty-one months during the years 1824–26. He became once more a proprietor in 1840 and was joined by 1854 by his son, William's share being transferred in 1864 to his father's associate in biblical study, the Baptist minister, the Reverend Fitzherbert Bugby (1823–87). After the death of John Rylands his widow became a proprietor in 1889.[39]

The library at Longford Hall was at the very least some six times as large as the one in John Rylands's London house which contained 325 volumes at the sale of 1908. Its stocks enabled him to pursue the aim of methodical self-improvement, and especially to

[37] *Manchester City News*, 15 April 1865, 3ii.

[38] JRL., Rylands Papers, *Catalogue of excellent modern furniture which will be sold by auction, by Capes, Dunn, & Co., on Monday June 29th 1908. . . on the premises, Longford Hall, Stretford* (Manchester: Sever, 1908, 103pp.).

[39] The share registers of the Portico Library were consulted in 1990 by kind permission of the Librarian, Mrs Janet Allan.

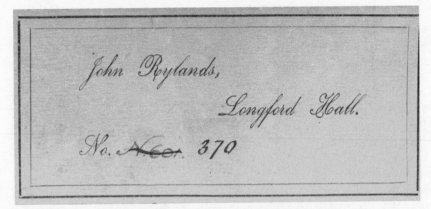

Figure 8: Bookplate of John Rylands, 1862

The plate is reproduced from the copy of *Pickwick Papers* (Chapman and Hall, 1862, with illustrations by Seymour and Phiz) held in the John Rylands Library. In its simplicity it provides a striking contrast to the armorial bookplate designed in 1894 for the John Rylands Library. The number 370 corresponds to the entry in the 1881 catalogue. Seven of the other eight of Dickens's novels held by the Library have a sequence of three numbers entered upon the plate: only two have two numbers. The deletion of the earlier numbers may imply the existence of two catalogues predating that of 1881.

(John Rylands Library)

develop his biblical interests. Those interests seem to have inspired him to add Greek to his Latin and French while his zeal for the propagation of the New Testament encouraged him to learn Italian. Always humble in his love of letters, he never became an intellectual, an aesthete or a bibliophile. He was interested in the content of books and not in their covers. His bookplate was a simple utilitarian rectangle, 4" x 2", bearing the number of the book below the inscription 'John Rylands, Longford Hall' (Fig. 8). Books as books held no interest for him. His special interest lay in religious literature rather than in first editions, fine bindings or the publications of private presses. In the outside world he established both mill libraries and mill schools. He also installed a book repository as well as a library in the town hall which he built for Stretford. From that depot he circulated amongst the poor thousands of books, both sacred and secular, of the highest and best class.[40] His aspirations always remained of the highest order. 'He had a great dislike and dread of unwholesome literature'.[41] He also made frequent and valuable contributions to the libraries of Sunday schools and of ministers of religion, for whom education was a sheer necessity.

[40] [S.G. Green] *In memoriam John Rylands* (1889), 33.
[41] Ibid., 70, quoting the Reverend J.W. Kiddle (1834–1911) at the memorial service on 16 Dec. 1888.

The contents of the library give an unusual insight into the life of a prosperous Victorian merchant, into his interests, into his habits and even into his personal history. It would be improper to scrutinize those contents with a jaundiced eye, suffused by what E.P. Thompson has termed 'the enormous condescension of posterity'. Nor would it be fair to judge them by the high standards set by Matthew Arnold, the contemporary prophet of culture, who divided English society into three orders, Barbarians, Philistines and Populace and who found the perfect type of Philistine in the unfortunate Thomas Bazley of Manchester (1797–1885). The library cannot be said to have been, in Arnold's definition, an assembly of 'the best that is known and thought in the world'. Nor was it a palladium of 'sweetness and light' in the phrase coined by Swift and popularized by Arnold. Its holdings do not however harmonize easily with the contents of the Palatine Library of the future envisioned in ironical vein, by Arnold in 1865:

Then, for the book-shelves. There will be found on them a monograph by Mr Lowe on the literature of the ancient Scythians, to revenge them for the iniquitous neglect with which the Greeks treated them; there will be Demosthenes, because he was like Mr Spurgeon: but, else, from all the lumber of antiquity they will be free. Everything they contain will be modern, intelligible, improving; *Joyce's Scientific Dialogues, Old Humphrey, Bentham's Deontology, Little Dorrit, Mangnall's Questions, The Wide Wide World, D'Iffanger's Speeches, Beecher's Sermons*; – a library, in short, the fruit of a happy marriage between the profound philosophic reflection of Mr Clay, and the healthy natural taste of Inspector Tanner.[42]

If we seek to apply Arnold's criteria to the library at Longford Hall we encounter difficulties. Those difficulties arise mainly from its failure to conform to Arnold's scornful standards. Thus the library, so far as we know, included nothing by Bentham, Mangnall, D'Iffanger or 'Old Humphrey' (one of six pseudonyms used by George Mogridge) and no scientific dialogues whatsoever. Admittedly it did hold works by Beecher and by Spurgeon together with *Little Dorrit* and at least one novel by the author of *The wide wide world*. It must however be remembered that Swift in 1697 had contrasted the 'sweetness and light' of ancient authors with the 'dirt and poison' of the moderns: the Longford Hall collection held copies of both Homer and Virgil, unaccompanied by any work of Demosthenes. Moreover the values of Matthew Arnold and of John Rylands seem to have been diametrically opposed. Arnold nourished a deep-rooted detestation of Dissent, of Manchester, and

---

[42] Matthew Arnold, *Essays in criticism* (Macmillan, 1865), xiii-xiv, Preface. James Clay (1805–73), M.P. for Hull (1847–73), advocated the study of modern science in education in place of Latin and Greek. Richard Tanner was a police inspector noted for his prompt action in crossing the Atlantic by steamer in 1864 in order to arrest a fleeing murderer. D'Iffanger was identified in 1968 by Sister Marion Hoctor as a misnomer for the Tory-Radical M.P., William Busfield Ferrand (1809–89).

of machinery. He lost all of his precious sweetness and light when he wrote about Dissent, which he equated with spiritual anarchy. He aspired to free the middle class from its estranging influence and to bring Dissenters into the mainstream of national life, a mainstream which he identified with State and Church. Such a mainstream could hold no attractions for John Rylands, who nourished only contempt for the State and who remained a generous supporter of the Anti-State Church Association, founded in 1844 in order to secure the disendowment of the Church of England. Undoubtedly Arnold's expression in 1865 of his own liberal Anglicanism was couched in extreme terms and was modified shortly thereafter: from all later reprints of the preface he excised the above-quoted passage. It would thus seem unjust to apply Arnold's strict criteria to the library at Longford Hall and to consign its contents to the rubbish heap of history. Perhaps it may be best simply to accept the library upon its own merits, as a collection built up by a busy man of affairs for his own purposes. The apparent contents may serve as one indicator, amongst others, of a very old-fashioned way of life.

Those contents may be broadly classified into four main categories: general works, literature, history and religion. The general works included two encyclopaedias[43] and four catalogues of the Portico Library (1831, 1845, 1856, 1863). Improving literature was a characteristic feature and may best be exemplified by such works as James Ferguson, *The pursuit of knowledge under difficulties*, and Sir Richard Phillips (1767–1840), *A million of facts* (1832). Such books were supplemented by Latin and Greek grammars, by *Familiar Latin quotations and proverbs* and by textbooks of geometry and algebra. Compendia of folk wisdom included Martin Tupper, *Proverbial philosophy (1838)* and *Laconics, or the best words of the best authors (1843,* 3 vols) by John Timbs (1801–75). What influenced John Rylands most were 'winged words'. He remained devoted to the perennial philosophy embalmed in the inherited wisdom of the ages and in the great tradition of past societies. Thus he always took a positive delight in imbibing the wisdom of others, whether in print or in speech: he loved aphorisms, epigraphs and mottoes and larded his formal addresses with quotations. A guide to conduct in society was available in *Etiquette for gentlemen with hints on the art of conversation* (1854). Another work probably dates from John Rylands's early days as a commercial traveller, J. Davies, *The innkeeper's and butler's guide* (1809). The medical history of the family may perhaps be reflected in four such works as Dr Thomas Jarrold, *Causes and prevention of curvature of the spine (1823),* James Braid, M.R.C.S.E., *Neuroypnology: or the rationale of nervous sleep*

---

[43] Abraham Rees, *Cyclopaedia of arts, science and literature* (1819, 45 vols). S.J. Coleridge, *Encyclopaedia Metropolitana* (second edition, 1848–58, 40 vols).

(1843), Joseph Constantine, *Handy book on hydropathy* (*1860*) and Dr A. Gentle, *Traité sur les sources ferrugineuses de Schwalbach* (1860). Spas and watering places seem to have ranked amongst the earliest resorts he visited, as is suggested by the presence of such works as J. Beck, *The Leamington guide* (? 1840), and Charles Braun, M.D., *The hot springs of Wiesbaden*, originally published in German in 1852–53. A small collection of travel literature indicates some of the places visited either by John Rylands or by members of his family and included guides to the Lakes by J. Otley (*1825*), to North Wales by Thomas Roscoe (1836), to the Isle of Wight by George Brannon (1834), to London by Francis Coghlan (1849), to Belgium and the Netherlands by Edmund Boyce (*1835*), to Italy by William Chambers (*1862*), to Jerusalem by W.H. Bartlett (*1855*) and W.K. Tweedie (*1859*) and to Egypt by W.H.D. Adams (*1867*). He also held two editions, published in 1837 and 1874, of a guide to French conversation by M. de Rouillons and Alfred Havet, together with ten French grammars.

The library held a host of works upon horticulture[44] and a number on various hobbies. John Rylands was no sportsman although he remained a keen billiards player, an interest reflected in Captain Crawley (G.F. Pardon), *Billiards for beginners: with the correct rules of the several games; and the true principles of the side-strokes familiarly and scientifically explained* (*1867*). Whether he made practical use of Grindon's *Manchester walks* (*1860*) is not known. A quasi-scientific pursuit is suggested by Jabez Hogg, *The microscope* (*1854*) and a domestic interest by Dr J.M. Bechstein, *Chamber and cage birds* (*1871*).

For relaxation in later life he or his wife turned on occasion to both magazines and to novels. The periodicals held by the library did not include any of the long runs of serial publications which remained a typical feature of the contemporary country house library: in particular it apparently excluded both the *Quarterly Review* and the *Edinburgh Review*. Its holdings comprised more popular fare such as *Bell's Weekly Messenger* (1796–1809, 14 vols), *Johnson's Penny Fireside Journal, a magazine of amusing and instructive literature* (*1843–45*, 3 vols), *Chambers's Miscellany* (1844, 4 vols) and *Household Words* (1850–59, 19 vols). The novels on the shelves may perhaps have been chosen by Martha Rylands. They included tales of a domestic and religious character, often written by lady novelists such as Charlotte M. Tucker ('A Lady of England' or

---

[44] Those works included two journals, George W. Johnson, *Gardener's Monthly Volume for 1857* (with nine out of twelve parts) and *Gardener's Chronicle and Agricultural Gazette*, 1856, 1857. Those periodicals were supplemented by such works as Peter Boswell, *The poultry yard* (1841), Frederick Falkner, *The muck manual for farmers* (*1843*), W. Jones, *The gardener's receipt book* (*1845*), *Beauties and wonders of vegetable life* (Religious Tract Society, 1866) and Leo Grindon, *Manchester flora* (*1859*).

'A.L.O.E.', represented by eight novels), Elizabeth Charles (with seven novels in the Schönberg-Cotta series) and Hesba Stretton (with six novels). The library did not apparently include any of the novels written by Mrs Radcliffe, by Jane Austen, by the Brontë sisters, by Mrs Gaskell, by Mrs Craik or by George Eliot who may have lost favour among believers after her translation of Strauss's *Leben Jesu*. There were however two of Harriet Beecher Stowe's minor tales but no *Uncle Tom's cabin* (1852), one novel by Mrs Henry Wood, *Bessy Wells* (*1875*), one by Mrs Linnaeus Banks, *The Manchester Man* (*1876*), one by Mrs Humphrey Ward, *Jasper Lyle* and finally *Daisy* (*1868*) by Susan B. Warner, the pseudonym used by Elizabeth Wetherell, author of *The wide wide world*. Into the same category fall one novel by Harrison Ainsworth, *The miser's daughter* (*1842*), three by Hawthorne, including *The scarlet letter* and *The house of seven gables*, one by George Sand, *Consuelo II* (1847) and one by Alexandre Dumas, *The lady with camelias* (*1848*). Children's novels included five penned by Annie Rylands and by Dora Rylands, who may well have been John's nieces.[45]

Classical literature was represented by Pope's *Iliad* (1736, 6 vols) and his *Odyssey* (1752, 5 vols) and by Dryden's Virgil (1697, 4 vols) but excluded the works of Herodotus, Thucydides, Polybius, Horace, Livy and Tacitus. European literature began for John Rylands in the seventeenth century with Cervantes, *Don Quixote* (in the 1792 edition of Smollett's translation). From Italy there was nothing by Manzoni or Alfieri and from France nothing by Corneille or by Molière. French literature was represented by Voltaire, *Zadig or the book of fate* (*1748*), by Rousseau, *Lettres écrites de la montagne* (1764) and by eleven novels written by Erckmann-Chatrian (*1865–73*) but not by anything from the pen of Balzac or Hugo. Germany was represented not by Schiller or Goethe but by Schlegel's, *The philosophy of history* (1846). From New England came not only tales by Hawthorne and by H.B. Stowe but also Longfellow's *Evangeline* and his *Poetical works*.

English literature began for John Rylands in the sixteenth century with the works of Shakespeare edited both by Pope (1728, 9 vols) and by Robert Inglis (*1864*), so excluding Chaucer. From the seventeenth century he held works by Milton, Bunyan, Locke

---

[45] Annie Rylands, *Left to take care of themselves* (1883); *The little world of school* (1885) *Jennie and her charges: or, True and false equality* (1887); *The two harvests* (1888). Dora Rylands, *Two little lives* (1885). Annie Rylands was the author of eight such novels, designed for use as Sunday School prizes. She does not appear in biographical dictionaries, either of women writers or of children's novelists. Whether she may be identified with the niece of John Rylands remains to be established. Anne, the niece, was however described as 'Annie' in the Probate Register for 1889, p. 330. None of Annie's first three novels, published in 1882 or earlier, was held at Longford Hall. All of the next four were so held, excluding only the last one published in 1891. Those four were not listed in the Reference Catalogue of the library but only in the Numerical Catalogue, on pp. 38, 42, 43 and 43(b).

and Dryden but nothing by Clarendon or Halifax. From the eighteenth century he had none of the writings of the Tories Swift and Johnson and none of those of the Whigs Addison, Gray or Collins. He did, however, have the poetical works of Young and of Cowper, together with Thomson's *The seasons*. The poetical works of Crabbe, Moore, Wordsworth and Byron were on his shelves but there was nothing by Blake, Keats, Shelley, Tennyson, Browning or even Palgrave. He acquired nine volumes of *The beauties of literature*, edited by Alfred Howard in 32 volumes (*1834–35*).[46] Amongst his novels were *Robinson Crusoe* (1778) and *Tom Jones* but none by Goldsmith or Richardson. He held an almost complete set of Scott's *Waverley Novels*, edited by Robert Cadell (1829–34, with 32 titles in 47 vols) and ten of Dickens's fifteen novels, together with Wilkie Collins, *The moonstone* (*1869*). The serial versions of *Hard times* and *North and South* had both been printed first in *Household Words*. Apparently he had none of the novels written by Disraeli, Kingsley, Hughes, Borrow, Reade, Trollope or Thackeray.

History began for him in the eighteenth century in so far as published history was concerned and in the sixteenth century in so far as recorded history was concerned. His collection included works written in the great Liberal tradition by Gibbon and Lecky. He held histories of England by Hume and Smollett (*1754–62*, 13 vols) and Macaulay (*1848, 1855*, 5 vols) and several classics of European history.[47] A continuing interest in military affairs was reflected in the presence on his shelves of four works, including one of general interest.[48] The more familiar field of textile history was represented by A.J. Warden, *The linen trade* (*1864*), Baines's *History of the cotton manufacture* (*1835*) and Ure's *Philosophy of manufactures* (*1835*) as well as his *The cotton manufacture of Great Britain* (*1836*). There were none of the works of Guest, Gaskell, Kay-Shuttleworth or Ellison. There were however three studies of the steam engine by Galloway (*1831*), by Lardner (*1836*) and by Hopkinson (*1854*). It may be reasonable to assume that John Rylands felt little need to secure moral support from Samuel Smiles and held copies of only two works by the learned doctor, *George Stephenson* (*1857*) and *Self-help* (*1859*) whereas Stretford Public Library in 1883 held fifteen works by Smiles. Specific economic concerns were however reflected in the presence of the

---

[46] The nine volumes were devoted respectively to Pindar and Goldsmith, Fénelon and Kotzebue, Sheridan and Fox, Fielding and Smollett, Erskine and Franklin, Hume and Robertson, Milton and Young, Swift and Gifford, Johnson and Hervey.

[47] W.R. Robertson's *History of Charles V* (*1769*) Motley's *Rise of the Dutch Republic* (*1856*) and W.H. Prescott's *Philip II* (*1855–58*).

[48] T.M. McNevin, *History of the volunteers of 1782* (1845), H.W. Bertie, *Address to the Second Essex Rifles* (*1865*), A.W. Kinglake, *The invasion of the Crimea* (*1863*) and William Stokes, *British war history during the present century* (*1869*).

leading anti-Corn Law periodical, in studies of the Cobden Treaty and of the Cotton Famine and in three depression-inspired tracts.[49]

Local literature included John Byrom's *Poems* (1773, 2 vols) as well as novels by Harrison Ainsworth and by Mrs Banks. Local history extended for him as far as Liverpool and was represented by *The club* (1824), Faucher's *Manchester in 1844*, Bamford's *Life of a radical (1841)*, Prentice's *History of the Anti-Corn Law League* (1853), *Liverpool life* (1856) and J.T. Slugg, *Reminiscences of Manchester fifty years ago (1881)*. The history of his family and his firm was touched upon in three publications, in D. Puseley, *The commercial companion (1858)*, in J. Harland, *Genealogy of the Pilkingtons of Lancashire* (edited by W.E.A. Axon and printed for private circulation in *1875*), and in H.R. Fox Bourne, *The romance of trade (1876)*.

Social questions were as strongly represented in the collection as economic affairs. John Rylands's interests in this sphere were practical rather than theoretical. Not one of the great trilogy discussing the condition of England question was listed in his catalogue i.e. *Past and present, Unto this last*, and *Culture and anarchy*. John Ruskin, *Selections from his writings (1861)* found its way on to the shelves but was unaccompanied by any offerings from Carlyle, Arnold, Martineau or even W.R. Greg. Rylands did however have some of the most relevant books of the day upon social questions. He remained most interested in the social problems of large cities, in the failings of the criminal law, the poor law and the Established Church and in the needs of fallen women, prisoners and, above all, orphans. A selection of typical titles in this sphere would include *The wilds of London (1874)* by James Greenwood, *Ten years in the slums (1879)* by Alfred Alsop, *Social wreckage (1883)* by Frances Peek, *Work among the lost (1870)* by J.E. Hopkins, *The perils of orphanland (1874)* by M.M. Robertson, *Children reclaimed for life (1875)* by J.H. Pike and *Cared for; or, the orphan wanderers (1881)* by Mrs C.E. Bowen. Two works on coffee rooms inspired him to take positive action and to found from 1883 non-sectarian temperance institutes.[50]

About one-third of the whole catalogue comprised religious works. The importance of religion was even greater than is suggested by this quantitative estimate. It is reflected in the

---

[49] *The League* (1843–46, 3 vols). H.R. Luck, *The French treaty and tariff of 1860 (1861)*. John Watts, *The facts of the cotton famine (1866)*. William Hoyle, *Our national resources (1871)*. Henri Cernuschi, *Monetary diplomacy in 1878 (1878)* and Ernest Seyd, *The decline of prosperity* (1879).

[50] Elizabeth Cotton, *Our coffee rooms (1876)*. E.T. Bellhouse 'The coffee house movement', *Transactions of the Manchester Statistical Society*, 1879–80, which was the only volume of the Society's transactions held in the library.

grouping of titles together under appropriate subject-headings. Some of the most important headings are as follows: Bible, Biblical, Christ, Christian, Gospels, Hymns, Popery, Prayer, Reformation, Religion, Scripture, Sermons, Sunday and Testament, together with Commentary and Notes (Figs 9, 10 & 11). The prominence of religious literature reflects the strong local demand for religious and theological literature which characterized the Manchester book market in the 1850s in sharp contrast to that of Liverpool. 'Religious books hardly find a purchaser in Liverpool, while at Manchester at the other end of the line, they are in high demand'.[51] It may also reflect the religious fervour of Mancunian Liberalism during the final phase of the Test Acts. It certainly reveals John Rylands's acquaintanceship with such local ministers as Birt, Parker, Green and McLaren. Above all, it reflects his personal interests and his unceasing search for the ultimate meaning of existence. Those interests were not primarily philosophical: he had copies of Bacon's *Essays* (*1840*) and of Locke's *Philosophical works* (*1843*) but nothing by Hobbes, Darwin, Spencer, or Huxley. His primary interest did not lie in theology or in doctrine, in ecclesiastical history or in church government. He shared with Sir Thomas Browne a dislike for 'those wingy mysteries in divinity, and airy subtleties in religion, which have unhinged the brains of better heads'. He could spare no time for the Higher Criticism of the Bible. And he remained unmoved by the controversies which raged between different warring sects. What most concerned him was the relationship between religion and daily life, that is morality rather than dogma. In his view morality had to be based upon Scripture and, above all, upon the New Testament.

His sympathies were eclectic and his interests extensive, despite the strong Nonconformist tinge. Any apparent omissions from the catalogue are at least as instructive as the holdings listed. He held none of the works by the founding fathers of the Baptist and Congregational traditions, as he lacked any of the works of Filmer or Hooker. From the seventeenth century he held the works of Bunyan and Baxter, especially *The saints' everlasting rest*, Samuel Butler, *Hudibras* and Jeremy Taylor, *The golden grove* (1836). He had two works by William Penn, *The traits of solitude* and *The rise and progress of the people called Quakers*. He also had his own copy of Joseph Butler, *The analogy of religion*, a work which was essential reading at Cavendish under Joseph Parker. Methodist influence affected his life indirectly through his early

---

[51] *The Times*, 9 Aug. 1851, 9iii, 'The literature of the rail', reprinted in Samuel Phillips, *Essays from 'The Times'* (Murray, 1851, 1871), i, 322 and quoted in W.M. Acworth, 'W.H. Smith and Son' in *English Illustrated Magazine*, Aug. 1892, 807.

Number. Published.

Number	Entry
66	Bible in Many Tongues, The; (see also No. 33.).
77	, Companion to the;
4	, Teaching and the Sabbath School; by Jas. Inglis.
7	, Pleasant Hours with the;
6	, Key to
150	, Help to reading the; by Benjm E. Nicholls. M.A.
218	& Modern Thought; by Rev. T.R. Birks M.A.
130	, Select Passages from the; by Alexr Adam
179	the best Teacher, The;
108	Introduction to the Study of the; by Geo: Tomline D.D.
264	A New . . . . ; . C.P. Burrows D.D.
193	Handbook; by Joseph Angus D.D.
1303	, Le Manuel de la; by Dr Joseph Angus.
·	, see separate Books, i.e. Genesis. &c, &c.
148	History, by Rev. Wm G. Blaikie, A.M.
200	Text Cyclopædia; by Rev. Jas Inglis
329	, The Superhuman Origin of the; by Henry Rogers
253	, The Prefaces to Luther's; by T.A. Readwin F.G.S.
169	Readings from the Gospels; by Mrs Fredk Locker
9	Readers, A Reference Manual for; by Wm R. Lyth
116/8	Sketches; by Rev. S.G. Green B.A. 3 Vols.
33	, Our English;
257	, The Villages of the; by Rev. Paxton Hood.
38	Prayers, The Book of; by John B. Marsh
39	An Index to the Holy; (Partridge's)
56	, Proverbs & Precepts from the;
320	Animals; by Rev. J.G. Wood M.A., F.L.S.
261	its own Interpreter, or the Christians' Manual.
1192	, The Plants of the; by Rev. John H. Balfour. M.A.
112	Biblical Liturgy, A; by David Thomas.
291	Cyclopædia; by Rev. John Eadie, D.D.
337	Atlas & Scripture Gazetteer.

Figure 9: Specimen page from the 1881 Library Catalogue, showing the entries under 'Bible' and 'Biblical'

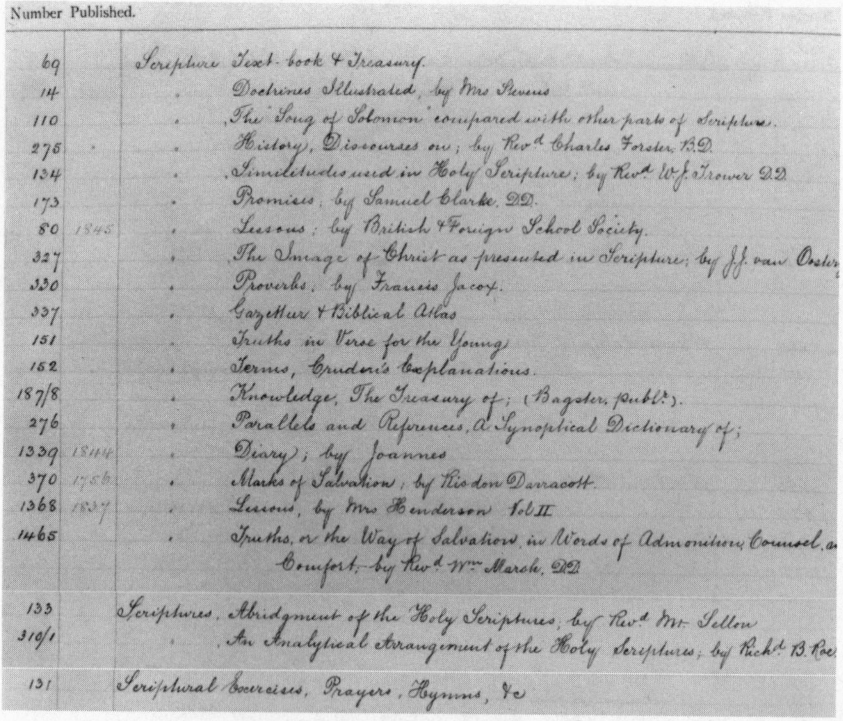

Number	Published.	
69		Scripture Text-book & Treasury.
14		. Doctrines Illustrated, by Mrs Stevens
110		. "The Song of Solomon" compared with other parts of Scripture.
275		. History, Discourses on; by Revd Charles Forster B.D.
134		. Similitudes used in Holy Scripture; by Revd W. J. Trower D.D.
173		. Promises; by Samuel Clarke, D.D.
80	1845	. Lessons; by British & Foreign School Society.
327		. The Image of Christ as presented in Scripture; by J.J. van Oster[zee]
330		. Proverbs; by Francis Jacox.
337		. Gazetteer & Biblical Atlas
151		. Truths in Verse for the Young
152		. Terms, Cruden's Explanations.
187/8		. Knowledge, The Treasury of; (Bagster, publr).
276		. Parallels and References, A Synoptical Dictionary of;
1339	1844	. Diary; by Joannes
370	1756	. Marks of Salvation; by Risdon Darracott.
1368	1837	. Lessons, by Mrs Henderson Vol II
1465		. Truths, or the Way of Salvation, in Words of Admonition, Counsel, a[nd] Comfort; by Revd Wm March, D.D.
133		Scriptures, Abridgment of the Holy Scriptures; by Revd Mr Sellon
310/1		. An Analytical Arrangement of the Holy Scriptures; by Richd B. Roe
131		Scriptural Exercises, Prayers, Hymns, &c

Figure 10: Specimen page from the 1881 Library Catalogue, showing the entries under 'Scripture' and 'Scriptural'

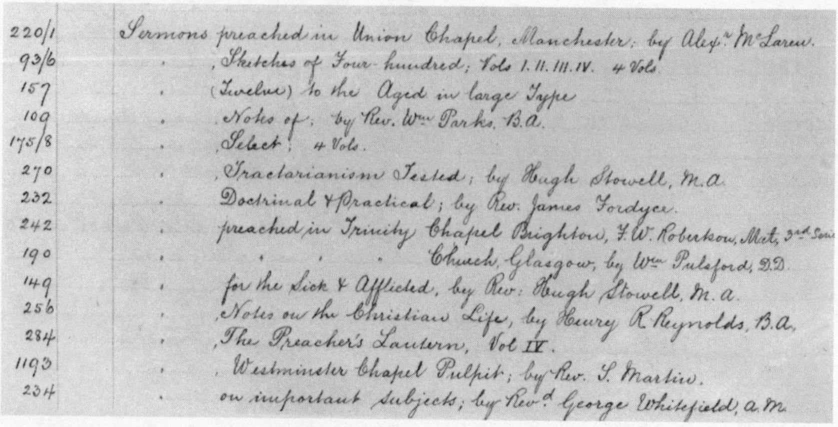

220/1	Sermons preached in Union Chapel, Manchester; by Alexr McLaren.
93/6	. Sketches of Four-hundred; Vols I. II. III. IV. 4 Vols.
157	. (Twelve) to the Aged in large Type
109	. Notes of; by Rev. Wm Parks. B.A.
175/8	. Select; 4 Vols.
270	. Tractarianism Tested; by Hugh Stowell, M.A.
232	. Doctrinal & Practical; by Rev. James Fordyce.
242	. preached in Trinity Chapel Brighton, F.W. Robertson, Met, 3rd Seri[es]
190	. . . . Church, Glasgow, by Wm Pulsford, D.D.
149	. for the Sick & Afflicted, by Rev: Hugh Stowell, M.A.
256	. Notes on the Christian Life, by Henry R. Reynolds, B.A.
284	. The Preacher's Lantern, Vol IV.
1193	. Westminster Chapel Pulpit; by Rev. S. Martin.
234	. on important Subjects; by Revd George Whitefield, A.M.

Figure 11: Specimen page from the 1881 Library Catalogue, showing the entries under 'Sermons'

(John Rylands Library, English Manuscript 1140)

association with the Calvinistic Methodists of North Wales and through his deep interest in hymns: he held John Wesley's *Moral and sacred poems* (*1744*) and Whitefield's *Sermons* (1833). He assimilated the best of the renascent Anglican tradition and approved of the staunch defence of Christianity undertaken by Paley in his *Evidences of Christianity* (*1797*) and in his *Natural theology* (*1802*). The great Evangelical revival had been stimulated by the influence of Wilberforce's *Practical view of the prevailing religious system of professed Christians* (*1797*). However, John Rylands held nothing by other members of the Clapham Sect. What apparently did arouse his interest was the Christian tradition of political economy, set forth notably by Thomas Chalmers in his *Discourses* and in his *Commercial discourses*: apparently he had no works by other representatives of this school of thought, such as Malthus, Copleston, Sumner or Whately. The great religious movements of the century hardly seem to be reflected in this collection. John Rylands had a copy of J.R. Beard, *The religion of Jesus Christ, defended from the assaults of Owenism* (1839) but nothing by the representatives of the Oxford movement or of the Christian Socialist movement. He had nothing written by Newman, Keble, Jowett or A.P. Stanley but he did have a copy of *Science and the Gospel, a series of essays* and a copy of Gladstone's *Vaticanism; an answer to reproofs and replies* (1875).

The library included works by the modern representatives of the Nonconformist and Presbyterian traditions.[52] The Baptist tradition was represented by 'the apostle of roast beef and racy religion' C.H. Spurgeon, in his *John Ploughman's talk or plain advice for plain people* (*1868*) and *The treasury of David* (vol. III only of 7 vols) and by S.G. Green, *Bible sketches* (*1865–70*, 3 vols) and *The written word* (*1871*). The same tradition was incorporated in the work of two local Baptist ministers, John Birt, author of *Patristic evenings* (*1846*) and Alexander McLaren (1826–1910), author of *Sermons preached in Union chapel, Manchester* (*1872*). Two other eminent local preachers were represented in the library. First, the charismatic Anglican and unofficial 'Bishop of Salford', Hugh Stowell (1799–1865) who enjoyed the unique distinction of having a church built specially for his ministry and having a memorial church named after him: his *Sermons for the sick and afflicted* were published posthumously, in 1866. Secondly, Dr Joseph Parker, who

52 Such works included William Stokes, *History of the Baptists and their principles* (Manchester, *1863*), T.S. James, *History of Presbyterian chapels and charities* (*1867*) and A.B. Grosart's *Representative Nonconformists* (*1879*), a study of the lives of John Howe, Baxter, Rutherford and Matthew Henry. James's work was entered in the catalogue as *The history of Presbyterian chapels and churches*.

was pastor at Cavendish from 1858 to 1869.[53] Other works by
Congregational pastors included books by John Waddington of
Stockport and three books by John Stoughton, minister at Hornton
Street, close to John Rylands's London residence in Kensington.[54]
Above all, one Congregationalist biography aptly epitomized the life
of John Rylands himself: *Ever working, never resting: a memoir of the
Revd John Legge Poore (1874)* by John Corbin. From such a bald
summary it would be presumptuous even for an ecclesiastical
historian to draw firm conclusions. We know some of the books he
owned but not all of them. We do not know which works he read or
which most influenced him. The literature so far scanned remained
marginal to the abiding preoccupations of John Rylands. His
interests remained primarily Scriptural and had been deepened
since the death of his son.

Having found comfort in the Scriptures since 1861, he
determined to make their treasures more readily accessible. He
therefore financed the compilation by two Baptist ministers of a new
edition of the Authorized Version of 1611 as 'a self-interpreting
Bible'. Towards the end of his long life he solemnly affirmed that
the Sacred Word had constantly proved 'the only answer to many
anxious questionings and the sure relief of innumerable cares' and
'his help in many difficulties, his consolation in many troubles, and
the source of all peace and hope to his soul' and that it contained
'the only, all-sufficient guidance to the Life Eternal'. He therefore
sought to enable any student to ascertain the sense of the Bible by
the best of all methods, that of self-interpretation. The governing
principle was one which had always proved the most fruitful
method of biblical study, that of 'explaining Scripture by Scripture,
without irrelevance or superfluity'. To secure that end the Rylands
Bible was arranged in 5,810 numbered paragraphs for perfect ease
of reference. Book, chapter and verse were still retained but were
superseded for the purpose of finding any particular passage by a
numbered paragraph. All paragraphs were listed in the index which
was a wholly original creation and served as the key to the whole
work, comprising a separate concordance of subjects as distinct
from words. That index was organized with ledger-like accuracy
and completeness. By its use any passage might be found almost
instantaneously with a great saving of time and pains. 'The
commercial experience of the Compiler had taught him the value of

---

[53] Works by Parker included *The working church (1857)*, *Emmanuel (1859)*, *Church
questions (1862)* and *Ecce Deus (1867)*, a response to Seeley's immensely popular *Ecce Homo*
(1865). John Rylands possessed a copy of the German translation of *Emmanuel* made by
L.T.H. Brönner and published by Stoffregen of Frankfurt in 1862: the British Library
Catalogue makes no mention of this edition.

[54] *Shades and echoes of Old London (1864)*; *Ecclesiastical history of England (1874)*; *Homes
and haunts of Luther (1875; R.T.S., 1883)*.

economising moments, in any matter requiring much turning of pages and comparison of various and distant points. . . The difference between the number of passages that can be found in a given time according to the present method, and in the ordinary chapter-&-verse plan of reference, will surprise almost all who make the experiment'. The organization of topics in the subject index made available a complete set of references under each heading. 'Many of the heads are doctrinal; and the summaries of Scripture teaching under each might serve to furnish a whole system of theology, not human, but Divine!'[55]

At this juncture it will be appropriate to be more specific about the limits of the 1881 Catalogue and to enumerate some works which were not entered in its pages but which John Rylands possessed. None of the following titles appear in the catalogue:

1. The three editions of the Rylands Bible (1863, 1878, 1886).
2. F.H. Scrivener's *Cambridge paragraph Bible* of 1873, which provided the basis for the editions of 1878 and 1886.
3. The two editions of the New Testament in Italian (1867, 1872) and in French (1869, 1870) which John Rylands sponsored.
4. The standard reference works by the six scholars who were singled out for specific mention in the preface to the Rylands Bible, i.e. Griesbach, Lachmann, Tischendorf, Tregelles, Hort and Westcott.
5. Cruden's *Concordance*, first published in 1737.
6. The collections of hymns published by John Rylands in 1864, 1885 and 1887.
7. Those hymnals which he specifically referred to in the preface to his own hymn book of 1885, i.e. those by E.H. Bickersteth, G. Thring, H. Allon and W.G. Horder, the last two being Congregational ministers.
8. His collections of psalms.
9. His reference works relating to hymnology.
10. Almost all of the 182 hymn books which were transferred in 1909 to the John Rylands Library, only eight being listed in 1881.

This long list of omissions might be extended by reference to such features as the apparent absence of any of the early volumes of Joseph Parker's *The people's Bible*, which began to appear in 1883, or of any dictionary whatsoever. Inevitably the list raises a host of questions, any answers to which must remain for the moment

---

[55] *The Holy Bible, containing the Old and New Testaments, arranged in paragraphs* (Chilworth: Unwin, 1886), Preface, v, viii. *An index designed to accompany the Holy Bible arranged in paragraphs* (Chilworth: Unwin, 1886), Preface, vi.

largely speculative. Perhaps the most intriguing of those questions relates to the function of the apparently empty Bookcase VI in the Billiards Room. Was this particular case really empty? Or did it serve to house works of the highest significance for John Rylands? Did it perhaps contain his own biblical library, which was deemed inappropriate for the mundane pages of a catalogue? And what was the ultimate fate of that particular collection? Moreover, some doubt remains about the specific function of those biblical works of reference which were apparently held outside the main stock and which were listed in the 1881 Catalogue. They include five works in particular: Henry Alford's *Greek Testament*, Alexander Cruden, *Explanations of Scripture terms (1840)*, *A synoptical dictionary of Scripture parallels and references (1851)*, R.B. Roe, *An analytical arrangement of the Holy Scriptures, according to the principles. . .of parallelism in Lowth, Jebb and Boys (1851, 2 vols)*, *An index to the Holy Bible* published by S.W. Partridge and Joseph Angus, *Le manuel de la Bible* (1854, translated into English in *1857*). Why were these works separated from the others? Were they duplicates? Had their value perhaps declined over time? These questions should be posed, even if they cannot yet be answered.

During the 1860s John Rylands's biblical studies extended his interests into the sphere of an older, a greater and a non-sectarian tradition. Already at Gorton in 1846 he had based his educational measures upon the twin foundations of Christianity and the Scriptures, scrupulously avoiding any denominational associations. During the next decade he became increasingly a lay apostle of the Church Universal, freed from the constraints of any single sect. That transition took place under the influence of two ministers, the Congregationalist Dr Joseph Parker from 1858 and the Baptist Dr Samuel G. Green (1822–1905), who was broad and catholic in his sympathies and wholly out of touch with 'narrow and unprogressive sectarianism'.[56] That new and proto-ecumenical trend is apparent in a number of ways, in his support of non-sectarian Christian societies, in his patronage of the New Union Church founded in 1864, in his employment in biblical research of that church's pastor, the Revd Fitzherbert Bugby,[57] as well as John Gaskin, reputedly a member of the Brethren, in his strenuous efforts to free the Bible from sectarian custody and to restore it to the individual reader, and in his publication of the *Cavendish hymnal* (1864). In 1861 he gave forceful expression to his own faith in the essential fellowship of all worshippers of Christ.[58] In 1864 his first great hymnal proudly proclaimed its indifference to 'the mere denominationalism of the

---

[56] *Baptist Handbook*, 1906, 441.

[57] *Manchester City News*, 28 May 1887, 6iv.

[58] *Our Own* i (1861), 113.

various authors'.[59] Not only did he remain convinced that national orthodoxy, as embodied in the Anglican Church, was simply superstition and vanity but he also came to believe that churches of every name had to be broken up so as to bring into a new harmony, by a natural process of rearrangement, men whose souls were in essence akin. Doubtless this wider vision of the true Church inspired his philanthropies of the next three decades. Paradoxically it may also have brought about his first encounter with the older Christian tradition of the Mediterranean world, the tradition of 'Christianity without the Bible'.[60]

His interest in Italy seems to have awakened from 1866, encouraged by the establishment of the Baptist mission in La Spezia and by the visit to Manchester of a Baptist missionary. James Wall (1837–1901) had first visited Italy in 1862 and served as a missionary in Bologna (1864–70).[61] In 1866 he first met John Rylands at Arthur Mursell's Baptist Chapel and was emboldened to ask him for 10,000 New Testaments in Italian.[62] John Rylands not merely promised him 20,000 copies but financed the publication in 1867 of an Italian translation by Giovanni Diodati and the distribution of 50,000 copies. So began a venture which was to strengthen the Baptist associations of one who was described by the Congregationalist Reuben Spencer as 'a staunch Nonconformist of the Baptist denomination, but . . . very catholic in his feelings to all other denominations'.[63]

6. The incorporation of Rylands & Sons Ltd and the continued expansion of its operations, 1873–87

John Rylands secured complete control over all of the firm's properties by means of two steps undertaken in 1871–72. First, he bought the full rights in the Wigan estates from his nephew, John R. Cross. Secondly, he terminated the partnership with Reuben Spencer. The death of his intended heir in 1861 and of his eldest son in 1872 had compelled him to provide for the future management of the concern on a more permanent basis. On 25 October 1873 the various properties held under the three names of Rylands & Sons, the Dacca Twist Company and the Manchester Wadding Company and valued at £1,024,788 were incorporated as a joint stock company. The name of Rylands & Sons Ltd preserved the name of the firm as it had been established in 1819 and reflected the hopes of the proprietor to perpetuate his name, if not his family. The nominal capital of £2,000,000 was fifty-fold the average capital

---

59 *The Cavendish hymnal* (1864), preface by Joseph Parker.
60 J.H. Shorthouse, *John Inglesant* (1881, 1891), 186.
61 *Baptist Handbook*, 1902, 215–18.
62 *Manchester City News*, 1 Jan. 1916, 7iii, A.H. King, '"Rylands's" fifty years ago'.
63 *Manchester City News*, 15 April 1865, 3ii.

of the firms then existing in the cotton industry[64] and formed the largest single capital therein until the creation of the Coats sewing-thread combine in 1896. Rylands & Sons Ltd was one of the thirty-one private limited companies registered in the cotton industry during the great joint-stock boom of 1873–75 but forged ahead of most large firms in seeking incorporation, being the fifteenth private limited company to be registered within the cotton industry since the first such incorporation in 1860. The new company extended the privilege of shareholding to its principal employees and clients in harmony with the contemporary enthusiasm for 'industrial partnership'. Thus 454 shareholders together held the initial issue of 64,036 £20 shares, of which 50,026 or 78.5 per cent were held by the 'Governor' of the company, the only member of the firm to draw no salary.

The transfer of private property was made in a 'very handsome and generous manner' and at great personal sacrifice. No charge was made for 'good will', although John Rylands might well have asked for £500,000.[65] The shares speedily rose to a premium. The firm preserved the separate identities of the enterprises operated under its three business-styles and thus did not unduly obtrude the full extent of its operations upon the public gaze. The adoption of the company form of organization gave the firm artificial immortality through the perpetual succession conferred by statute and enabled Rylands to provide for its future management by appointing as directors Reuben Spencer in 1873 and William Carnelley (1821–1919) in 1874. It also made possible the use of shares and, from 1889, of debentures as instruments of industrial finance.

No change took place in the style of management. John Rylands did not place his office in commission and devolved no power whatsoever to the board of directors as a board. He was in fact specifically entrusted by the articles of association with supreme power within the company and remained unique in having his own Minute Book. Those articles of association were discovered in 1890 to be 'at variance in so many points with Stock Exchange requirements' that a quotation could not be granted.[66] In any case John Rylands held the overwhelming majority of the initial issue of shares. Thus he continued to manage the affairs of the firm after 1873 as beforehand. He did foil an apparent attempt by Reuben Spencer to enhance his own role by summoning five board meetings

[64] *Textile Manufacturer*, 15 June 1877, 183 estimating the average capital of 1,453 firms at £39,573.

[65] JRL., Archives of Rylands & Sons Ltd., General Meetings Minute Book, 2, 21 Feb. 1874; 214, 7 Feb. 1896, W. Carnelley.

[66] JRL., Archives of Rylands & Sons Ltd., Board of Directors Minute Book, i, 245, 22 March 1890.

during the three months of February, March and April 1874. After returning from a tour of Europe John Rylands held one brief meeting of the board on 21 May 1874[67] and thereafter held no more for almost three years. No recorded meetings of the board took place for the six years between 1 March 1877 and 12 March 1883.[68] Nor did any take place for another three years after 1883 until 5 March 1886. In sum John Rylands held only fourteen short meetings of the board during the fourteen years 1873–1886. Thus he doomed to frustration future scholars seeking insight into the business history of the firm by consulting the minutes of the board before the year 1887.

A new wave of expansion followed the incorporation of the firm and was partly financed by the windfall-gains which accrued during the Coal Famine of 1872–73. The output of the Wigan collieries during those years raised the firm's returns to new heights in harmony with the increased price of coal. In London the firm's operations had remained comparatively limited for its first twenty-five years. Its warehousing facilities in the capital expanded in three main phases, in 1864–65, in 1869 and, above all, in 1874–75 when the London office became a major branch of the firm. In 1874 it concluded an advantageous contract with its landlords, the Company of Curriers. Thereunder it built a new hall for the Company and secured in return the invaluable right to extend and consolidate its premises.[69] The Company admitted John Rylands to its freedom on 17 November 1874 and so strengthened a profitable association between landlord and tenant. In Manchester the sale in 1873 of Dacca Mills, to make way for the railway-extension which was opened to Central Station by the Cheshire Lines Committee in 1877, was one of the most profitable transactions in real estate ever undertaken by the firm. Thereafter the Irwell Works were renamed the Dacca Mills (Fig. 7) and the manufacture of grey Dacca calicoes was concentrated at the Gidlow and Gorton mills, supplemented by a small mill leased in 1876 at Crawshawbooth in Rossendale. In 1874 the firm had bought five more factories, Great Bridgewater Street Mills in Manchester, Swinton Mills, Primrose Mill at Walkden Moor, Waterloo Mills at Chorley and Hulme Street Mills in Manchester but declined to purchase a bleach works in Belfast. In 1875 it bought the large Mather Street and Fletcher Street Mills in Bolton (Fig. 12), to which district it returned for the first time since the abandonment of the Ainsworth mills after a destructive fire in 1868.[70] The firm used those new works in order

---

[67] Ibid., i, 8, 21 May 1874.

[68] Ibid., i, 11–12.

[69] E. Mayer, *The curriers and the City of London: a history of the worshipful company of curriers* (Worshipful Company of Curriers, 1968), 161–3.

[70] J. Clegg, *Annals of Bolton* (Bolton Chronicle, 1888), 116.

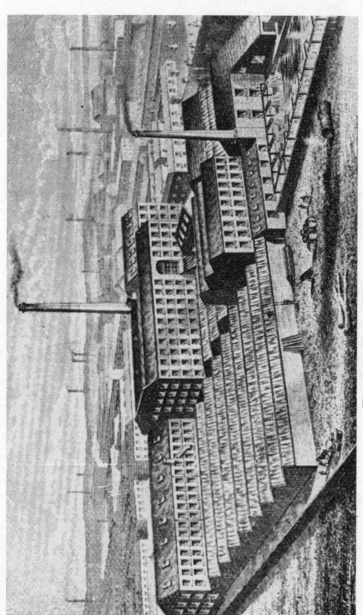

Figure 12: Bolton Mills, c. 1890

The Mather Street and Fletcher Street Mills were built in the 1830s and acquired by the firm in 1875. That investment proved to be unfortunate. The mills were old, the looms were old, wages were high and production remained a high-cost operation. The mills could not be integrated into the commercial structure of the firm. Their products were fancy cloths and competed with the products of the firm's own customers. Such fabrics could not be distributed by the firm and accumulated in stock so that the mills remained unprofitable. Two-thirds of their yarn had to be sold in the open market. Their sale was recommended in 1890 but was not effected until 1902. Even then it proved difficult to extract the price from the purchaser, Hollas & Farnworth, so that the sale contract became in effect for four years a hire-purchase agreement.

(The Guildhall Library, Commerce, 5 July 1893, 21)

to expand into the manufacture of floor-cloth, furniture, fancy cloths and dress goods. It manufactured floor-cloth at Chorley, shirtings and coloured goods at Swinton, packing-cases and furniture at its Hulme Street Works, clothing at the nearby Longford Mills and a whole range of fancy cloths upon 600 Jacquard looms at Bolton while its Medlock Works manufactured pattern cards as well as paper boxes, handled all its printing and letterpress work, especially the production of circulars for drapers, and so made it independent of outside printers.

Finally, the firm moved beyond the secure confines of the domestic market. By 1865 it had already employed one traveller for Holland and another for Canada. By 1875 it mustered thirty-nine departments and was ready to conquer new worlds: it changed its designation in the London directories from 'Manchester warehousemen' in 1874 to 'General Warehousemen' in 1875. From 1874 under the impetus of Spencer it launched from its newly expanded base in London an export drive, which was extended in 1876. Offices were opened in Paris and Montreal in 1874. The firm waged an aggressive price-cutting campaign in order to establish its name abroad and especially made a great push for business in Paris, displaying 'great determination to cut down all opposition'.[71] Agencies were also established in Constantinople in 1875, in Rio in 1876, in Genoa in 1877 and in Lyons, Rouen, Alexandria and Barbados in 1879. From 1879 Rylands & Sons embarked on a wave of imperial expansion, establishing agencies in Madras in 1879 and in Port Elizabeth in 1883. It began to display its wares at international exhibitions and to win prizes at Cape Town in 1877 and at Paris in 1878. Its entry into the direct shipping trade alarmed established merchant exporters. Early attempts to enter the trade to India, in 1879, in 1887 and in 1888, coincident with an attempt to tap the market of Japan, did not however prosper until 1904.[72]

The final phase of expansion took place in 1880–81. A second Gidlow Mill was opened at Wigan in 1880 for the manufacture of Dacca calicoes and maintained the high standards of architecture and production set by the first. Manufacturing operations were also extended in London where the firm acquired in 1874 a factory for the manufacture of shirts in Commercial Road, supplemented in 1881 by a factory for clothing-manufacture in Bethnal Green. Thus was completed the construction of the most colossal commercial power originating during the first quarter of the nineteenth

[71] Guildhall Library Manuscripts, Kleinwort, Sons & Co., Information Books, No.184, 76, quoting E. Ashworth & Co. of Manchester, 10 Nov. 1876, a reference for which I am indebted to Dr S.D. Chapman of the University of Nottingham.

[72] JRL., Archives of Rylands & Sons Ltd., Board of Directors Minute Book, i, 36, 24 Sept. 1887; 43, 22 Oct. 1887; 53, 10 Dec. 1887; 56, 16 Jan. 1888; 72, 24 March 1888.

century.[73] As John Rylands entered on the eighth decade of his life he began to slacken the pace of his activity. His achievement was greater than that of any contemporary businessman. From small beginnings he had built up the greatest of firms and had succeeded to the position of leadership formerly held by Arkwright, by Peel and by Horrocks within a much smaller industry. The organization of 200,000 spindles and 5,000 looms in seventeen mills represented the most extensive factory system under the control of a single firm and the greatest creation by any single entrepreneur within the textile industries. The firm stood somewhat apart from other large concerns because it was more important as a merchant and converter than as a manufacturer and more important as a

Table 1: Number of Employees of Rylands & Sons Ltd, 1840–1935

Year	Total	Manchester warehouse	Source
1840		28	
1847		under 100	
1860	2,000 plus		D. Puseley, *The commercial companion* (1860), 154
1865	4,500	600	*Manchester City News*, 15 April 1865, 3i
1875	nearly 12,000		H.R. Fox Bourne, *The romance of trade* (1876), 223; *Momus*, 15 May 1879, 81
1887	11,000–12,000		*British Trade Journal*, 1 April 1887, 278; *Manchester Courier*, 3 May 1887; J. Burnley, *The romance of modern industry* (1889), 270–1
1888	12,000	1,100	*Manchester of today* (1888), 79
1889	12,000		*In memoriam John Rylands* (1889), 34; *The century's progress: Lancashire* (1892), 73; W.A. Shaw, *Manchester old & new* (1894), ii, 39, gives 15,000
1897	12,300	1,200	R. Spencer, *History of Lancashire* (1897), 192, 236
1905	9,000	1,500	*Manchester Courier*, 1 Aug. 1905, 10i; JRL., Rylands & Sons Archives, General Meetings Minute Book, 329–30, 5 Aug. 1904
1909	8–9,000		*Illustrated London News Supplement*, 10 July 1909, xxii
1920	8,000 plus		JRL., Archives of Rylands & Sons Ltd, Minutes of the Board of Directors, vi, 421–2, for Prospectus dated 28 June 1920
1935	8,000		*The Red Book of Commerce* (1913–39)

[73] *The century's progress: Lancashire* (1892), 73.

manufacturer than as a spinner. Its spindles were exceeded in number by nine other firms but its looms by none, not even by Horrockses or Hoyle's. In manufacture, in finishing and in distribution Rylands & Sons had become 'the recognized and undisputed head and leader of the cotton trade' and 'the monarchs of the cotton industry of England'.[74] Its commercial operations dwarfed its manufacturing activities, generated an annual income greater than that enjoyed by many sovereign states, and had been paralleled in extent only in the most flourishing days of the East India Company.[75] As the master-builder of the largest textile house in the world[76] John Rylands had become 'the Wellington of commerce',[77] 'the old Field-Marshal of the Home Trade',[78] 'the Cotton King'[79] and 'the greatest merchant prince the world has ever seen'.[80]

7. The bases of the firm's commercial primacy

It was impossible for any single firm to acquire a monopolistic position in an industry where firms were numerous and generally small. The cotton industry had become so extensive that even the largest enterprise controlled only a minute fraction of the total manufacturing plant. Rylands & Sons controlled in 1873 only 3.5 per cent of the industry's capital and operated in 1888 only 0.5 per cent of the industry's spindles and 0.8 per cent of its looms. It had made its way against stout and ever renewed opposition, defying the established conventions of the trade and incurring the hostility of other firms. As a commercial traveller John Rylands had declined to join his fellows in carousing of an evening: as a merchant he repeatedly refused to conform to the customary practices of other merchant houses in Manchester. Rylands & Sons may not be regarded in any respect as a representative cotton manufacturing firm. It was set apart from the rest by its immense size, by its combination of spinning with weaving, finishing and merchanting, by its wide range of ancillary activities, by its vertical extension into the clothing industry and the thread trade, by its dependence upon the home market and by its lack of any mills in the most typical factory towns of Lancashire. Two features remain remarkable about the history of this firm: first, its simple survival in the slaughter house of the Manchester market and secondly, its successful expansion in the face of constantly renewed opposition.

[74] *Manchester of today* (1888), 79.
[75] *British Trade Journal*, 1 April 1887, 277.
[76] *Manchester Examiner*, 12 Dec. 1888, 5v.
[77] *Cotton Factory Times*, 14 Dec. 1888, 7iii.
[78] *Manchester City News*, 15 Dec. 1888, 5ii.
[79] *The Young Man*, April 1893, 111.
[80] *Commerce*, 5 July 1893, 17.

The causes of the successful expansion of that one great firm are to be found mainly in the unresting enterprise of one man, who 'accepted his work and calling as divine'[81] and approaches the ideal type of the dedicated entrepreneur inspired by other-worldly ideals. John Rylands concealed remarkable abilities beneath a wholly deceptive exterior,[82] (Figs 13–16) being small in stature and unimpressive in appearance, in speech or in gaze. 'You are respected most by those who know you best'.[83] Reticent in self-expression, simple in his language and averse to loquacity, he regarded discretion and secrecy as the key to success in business: he disliked idle chatter and addressed his shareholders with short but pithy speeches. Throughout life he remained unaffected and unassuming in demeanour: he claimed neither ancient gentility for his family nor a spurious antiquity for his firm. He nevertheless possessed almost superhuman mental and physical powers,[84] manifested in an irresistible energy, a great capacity for physical endurance and for unflagging industry, a genius for concentration and a power of rigid self-control. He never missed a single day in his regular attendance to business and at the age of seventy-five arrived punctually at the office at 8 a.m. in order to begin a twelve-hour working day in the office he shared with two secretaries. His sedulous desire to excel others in all he undertook may have stemmed from a wish to compensate for his physical shortcomings, from a sense of rivalry with his elder brothers or from a certain indisposition for social life but mainly originated in his upbringing at the hands of the mother whom he revered to the end of his days. 'Often has he told the writer [Reuben Spencer] that he owes nearly all he has to his mother's excellent practical common sense, wisdom, prudence, and ceaseless anxiety for the welfare of her family, as well as the formation of their characters, by the inculcation of the sublime principles of "pure and undefiled religion".'[85] More than fifty years after his mother's death John Rylands recalled in public her influence. 'At the mention of his mother his heart swelled with emotion, and he who had toiled and succeeded, amid difficulties and trials which would have crushed most men, stood there before that meeting with tears in his eyes, incapable for the moment of expression'.[86] In youth he channelled his energies into the field of commerce, where early success created a self-reinforcing disposition

[81] [S.G. Green], *In memoriam John Rylands* (1889), 54, memorial sermon delivered by S.G. Green on 16 Dec. 1888.

[82] *The Young Man*, April 1893, 111, Joseph Parker.

[83] [S.G. Green], *In memoriam John Rylands* (1889), 31–33, quoting from the address presented on the occasion of his commercial jubilee on 22 December 1873.

[84] *Manchester City News*, 1 April 1865, 3i.

[85] *Manchester City News*, 8 April 1865, 2vi.

[86] R. Spencer, *The home trade of Manchester* (1890), 175, referring to the address in 1883 at the annual meeting of the firm's benevolent society for packers and porters.

Figure 13: John Rylands in 1869

Portrait of John Rylands Esq., presented to Mrs Rylands by Managers of Departments and Commercial Travellers connected with the house of Rylands & Sons; Manchester, March 1869. The book shown beneath the left hand may be the first edition of the Rylands Paragraph Bible of 1863. The portrait was presented to Martha Rylands and was transferred by Enriqueta Rylands to the John Rylands Library, where it remained concealed from public view until 1972. It is now housed in the main library of the University of Manchester. The head and shoulders have been reproduced in the frontispiece.

(John Rylands University Library of Manchester)

Figure 14: John Rylands in 1879
A cartoon by the comic artist W.G. Baxter (1855–88)
(Momus, vol. 3:63, 15 May 1879, 8, 'Our album: John Rylands Esq.')

Figure 15: John Rylands in 1887

The picture is marked 'Artist's First Proof. H. Hills' and was engraved by Benyon & Co. of Cheltenham. Presumably Hills based the portrait upon 'a beautifully executed life size photograph of Mr. Rylands' which was presented by Mrs Rylands to the firm for display in the boardroom. 'Every director appreciates and regards with special admiration the expression in the Countenance'. (JRL, Archives of Rylands & Sons Ltd, Minutes of the Board of Directors, i, 31, 3 Sept. 1887; 49–50, 26 November 1887)

The present location of the photograph is unknown, as is that of another portrait. A large picture in colour of John Rylands was made by A. Debenham of Ryde and presented to the firm in 1889, at the request of Mrs Rylands. The directors accepted the coloured portrait for the New High Street boardroom and sent the plain portrait of 1887 to their London office (JRL, Archives of Rylands & Sons Ltd, Minutes of the Board of Directors, i, 166–7, 11 May 1889)

(John Rylands Library)

Figure 16: John Rylands in 1887
The original photograph is inscribed 'Yours Truly, John Rylands'. Its present location is
unknown.
([S.G. Green], In memoriam John Rylands (1889), frontispiece)

towards a business career. Thereafter he avoided any wasteful dissipation of his powers in other less profitable fields through systematic and continuous concentration of effort.

John Rylands was not prepared to sacrifice the welfare of his firm to the pursuit of a political career and found ample scope for the exercise of administrative, legislative and judicial functions within the sphere of his own business. He declined to become either a member of the Manchester City Council in 1838 or a county magistrate in 1845. Nor did he ever seek election as an M.P. He did not even become a director of the Manchester Chamber of Commerce and certainly never presumed to act as a public spokesman for the cotton industry, as Bazley did in the 1850s and Macara in the 1890s. Within that trade he promoted no cotton spinning or manufacturing companies and joined none of the syndicates of promoters formed for speculative mill-floating in the factory towns of Lancashire. He abstained from investing money either in the joint-stock limiteds of Lancashire or in overseas enterprises. He held shares in some ten companies, all local in origin, with the largest holdings in the District Bank and in the Equitable Fire Insurance Company, of which he became a local director.[87] He preferred county to civic honours: he served as a county magistrate from 1869 but shrank from sitting on the bench. When confidential information reached the City of London that he was worth two to three millions,[88] he was invited in 1878 to accept nomination as the sheriff of London. That office would have made him eligible to become the lord mayor of London but would inevitably have diverted some of his wealth from Manchester. He declined the offer. He took no active part in any of the great political, social or religious movements of the century and never became a public figure. No national honours were conferred on him and he died as he had lived, a commoner.

In his business activity he preferred to regard himself as a manufacturer, professing scorn for the pure merchant and contempt for mere publicity. He was nevertheless a born merchant who delighted in buying and selling well. If it be true that 'every one lives by selling something' then it must be conceded that John Rylands excelled all of his Manchester contemporaries in his skill at selling. He did so by maintaining absolute secrecy about his business operations, especially in regard to prices. His imagination remained large and vital, combining a comprehensive view of a vast field of operations with a minute care for detail. His quickness of

---

[87] The editor of the *Directory of Directors*, 1882, 359 and 1885, 286, may perhaps have confused John Rylands of Manchester with John Rylands of Warrington (1815–98).

[88] Guildhall Library Manuscripts, Kleinwort, Sons & Co., Information Books No.184, 76, quoting the report of Yates Bros of Manchester on Rylands & Sons Ltd, 10 Nov. 1876, a reference for which I am indebted to Dr S.D. Chapman.

perception and immense fertility of resource made him highly adaptable to changing conditions of trade and ever ready to make innovations, abandoning traditional practices with zest but always providing for the unknown and the uncertain. Consistently profiting from his own errors of judgement, he professed to have made more mistakes than any man in Manchester. His quasi-military capacity for command, dating from childhood, developed in maturity to a superb flair for organization. He became one of the most successful commercial administrators of all time and insisted on the indispensable need for the rigorous and constant control of costs. In his account books each department of the firm had to stand upon its own feet and could not expect to be subsidized by any other. He loved arithmetic, the compilation of tables of statistics of discount, interest and cloth-prices and the costing of labour-saving contrivances. By making accounting the focal technique of his business he imbued his employees with his own sense of the value of methodical organization. A keen observer of men and a dedicated listener, he revealed exceptional judgement in the selection of his managers. Indeed he attributed his success to the ability to read character, which secured him able and loyal servants.[89]

He made skilful use of his capital resources and consistently sought small profits from quick returns. He aimed to turn over his stock at least five times in each year and sought 'to make two per cent on our returns five times a year'.[90] Undoubtedly he benefited by the windfall gains accruing from fortunate investments made in real estate. His policy of strict frugality in personal expenditure led him to avoid any unnecessary expense in business and to abstain from conspicuous corporate consumption. Thus he never moved his warehouses from their original site to a more prestigious location, although from 1873 he did lease premises in Portland Street and so became landlord to a number of merchant shippers. He consistently preferred old to new mills. He profited from the depressions of 1837–42 and 1865–69 in order cheaply to acquire more factories and from the depressions of 1874 and 1879 in order to secure a reduction in the assessment of the Gidlow Works to the poor-rate of the Wigan Union.[91] By restricting dividends to a regular 5 per cent he ploughed back a very high proportion of profits into the business. By depreciating the ledger-value of warehouses, works and plant he built up a substantial but invisible reserve-fund. In the purchase of property he developed a number of

[89] B.T. Leech, 'Old Stretford. Recollections of half a century. V.-Bygone characters', *Manchester City News*, 23 Oct. 1909, 3iii, reprinted in *Old Stretford: reminiscences of the past half-century* (*Manchester City News*, 1910), 18.

[90] JRL., Archives of Rylands & Sons Ltd, General Meetings Minute Book, 20, 9 Dec. 1875, John Rylands.

[91] *Textile Manufacturer*, Aug. 1879, 264; Dec. 1880, 434.

useful techniques which greatly reduced the expenditure of cash and profited by the firm's growing prestige as the leading enterprise within England's leading industry. Thus he often persuaded vendors to lend back to the firm the monies they had only just received. Such loans would be secured against an interest-bearing mortgage on the property concerned. The repeated mortgage and re-mortgage of properties became in fact his most widely-used device for raising funds cheaply and for economizing on capital. Sometimes he induced vendors to accept shares as part of the purchase-price. On one rare occasion he offered the vendor of Swinton Mills a seat on the board where he remained from 1875 until his death in 1890. Operating costs were reduced through the manifold economies open to a vertically-integrated firm, by the strict avoidance of any use of credit, by the regular purchase of goods for cash and by the exaction of a full discount thereon, as a symbol of status as much as a saving of money.[92] Transport costs were reduced by the strategic location of each works near a railway, especially in the great junction-towns of Wigan, Bolton and Manchester. Labour costs were reduced by the employment of women as mule-spinners and in the manufacture of cloth and of clothing, especially in those towns where men were engaged in coal-mining, in engineering or on the railways. They were further controlled by the adoption of cost-cutting technical innovations which gave the firm the dual advantage of a modern plant within older buildings and enabled it to resist dictation of policy, even by the most powerful of trade unions. John Rylands blamed trade combinations for the depression of 1877–79, prophesying that 'unless some check were bought to bear upon them the prosperity of the country would be undermined and the trade of England ruined'.[93] The advantages the firm offered to employees generally spared it the affliction of strikes. At Gorton however it began to spin finer counts and conceded payment under the Stockport list but suffered in 1882 a strike by twenty self-acting mule minders for a 5 per cent advance. The firm first locked out all 1,200 hands and then replaced fourteen of the discontented minders either by piecers or by minders recruited from outside Gorton, including three women from its Wigan mills in a distinct encroachment upon a traditional sphere of male labour.[94] The aristocrats of the spinning-room were defeated in their attempt to exploit their key position to extort an increase in wages. The strike was a most exceptional incident in the history of a firm which proved able to win devoted and lengthy service from its employees.

[92] R. Spencer, *The home trade of Manchester* (1890), 69.
[93] JRL., Archives of Rylands & Sons Ltd, General Meetings Minute Book, 46, 4 Feb. 1878, John Rylands.
[94] *Gorton Reporter*, 12 Aug. 1882, 8ii; 19 Aug., 8ii.

As a vertically-integrated enterprise, Rylands & Sons was virtually self-sufficient and controlled all the processes of manufacture from the import of cotton to the sale of the finished product. Unlike other great firms it maintained no cotton-broking, marketing, shipping or banking affiliates but it made some and repaired most of its own machinery and engines at Gidlow and Gorton and even owned farms at Gidlow, Skelmersdale and Heapey. Its large size secured to it all the advantages accruing from the economies of scale in purchase, in manufacture and in sale. It spread its overhead costs by increasing the range of articles in which it dealt. It did not try to enter any branch of trade in which it could not succeed and indeed excel in price or in quality: it won a special reputation for its Dacca calicoes, for its bleached goods with their 'Heapey finish' and even for its Dacca and Longford sewing cottons. That reputation it maintained through the diligent branding of its products and the vigilant prosecution of piratical plagiarists of its marks. During the seven years after 1879 the firm registered some 433 trade marks, including 139 for cotton manufactures.[95] Amongst those marks were the Pilkington scytheman and the Rylands family motto 'Not the last', which also appeared on the company seal and on its letterheads.

Thus it secured some protection from the incidence of depression in any one field, remained largely unperturbed by cyclical fluctuations and never passed a year without making a profit in a trade noted for the regularity and the amplitude of its fluctuations. In the finishing processes it concentrated on dyeing and bleaching rather than on calico-printing in harmony with its original association with the linen trade. It pioneered the large-scale development of the ready-made clothing trade in Manchester, made its Longford Works from 1872 into the largest clothing factory in the city, employing 1,200 hands, and acquired the nearby Midland Works for use as a warehouse and making-up place for such clothing. Thus it controlled a whole bloc of factories in the district of Medlock, between Oxford Street, Cambridge Street, Hulme Street and Chester Street, which became comparable in importance to its works at Gorton and Gidlow. Finally, the Gidlow collieries employed male labour, supplied fuel to the firm's mills and eliminated the profits and freight of the coal merchant: they also provided a substantial surplus, especially of domestic coal, for sale and enabled the firm to become coal merchants in Wigan, Liverpool and West Lancashire.

One great external advantage enjoyed by the firm was the growing centralization of the home trade in 'Cottonopolis' which took place between 1830 and 1860 under the influence of the

[95] JRL., Archives of Rylands & Sons Ltd., Register of Trademarks (1886, 160pp.).

railways. By improving the range and quality of its products and by trebling the number of its travellers, from nineteen in 1865 to seventy in 1897, when S. & J. Watts mustered only thirty-six, it won the custom of many of the shrewdest and most able traders in the country in the drapers, enabling them to secure all their needs from one house and through one account. The loyalty of its clients was preserved by the tradition of absolute integrity in all his dealings maintained by John Rylands, by his steadfast refusal to sell direct to the public and even by the offer from 1873 of shares in the firm, which thus returned some of its profits to its customers. In time of bad trade as in 1878–79 the firm was prepared to lend its clients money against the security of such shares.

As the leading home-trade house it benefited by the greater proportionate value of the home trade in comparison to the export trade and by the relatively faster expansion of the home market after the depression of 1877–79. Even after Manchester lost its quasi-monopoly of distribution within the textile trade during the 1880s Rylands & Sons displayed the resilience of true enterprise. Its continued success contrasted sharply with the declining fortunes of other houses[96] and testified to its ability to develop those branches of trade thitherto neglected in the city, such as ready-made clothing, mantles, boots and shoes, carpets and furnishings.[97] The firm increased the number of its departments by one-fifth to forty-two by 1887, against the thirty-two departments of S. & J. Watts, in accordance with its aim to supply all dry goods, 'any articles, excepting, of course, such bulky articles as coals – which can be required by man, woman, or child, from birth to death, for their persons or their homes . . . but not soft goods, that is, provisions'.[98] The Manchester warehouses expanded in size to form four immense blocks parallel to the city's main centre of retail trade in Market Street. In 1897 they employed 1,200 hands, or one-tenth of the firm's labour-force, and handled an annual turnover of over £3,000,000 from 20,000 customers.[99]

Two-thirds of the firm's goods were sold at home and one-third abroad. Supplies were secured from all the producing centres of England and of Europe since the policy of free trade had made Britain one great free market for the goods of all nations. Exports

[96] *Manchester City News*, 13 Oct. 1888, 5iv, 'The Manchester home trade: present position and future prospects'; 20 Oct., 6v–vi; 27 Oct., 4iii–iv, 5ii–iv; 3 Nov., 5i–iii; 10 Nov., 5i–iii; 17 Nov., 5i; 24 Nov., 4v–vi; 1 Dec., 4vi–5i; 8 Dec., 4iv–v, 'A review of the home trade question'.

[97] Ibid. 27 Oct. 1888, 5ii; 5 Nov., 5i Home trader, 'Undeveloped branches of the home trade', reprinted in revised form in Home Trader [Reuben Spencer], *The home trade of Manchester* (1890), 45–73, 'Manchester home-trade houses' and in R. Spencer, *History of Lancashire*, (1897), 92–113.

[98] R. Spencer, *The home trade of Manchester* (1890), 52.

[99] R. Spencer, *History of Lancashire*, (1897), 192.

were sold either through Manchester merchants with good foreign connections or through foreign merchants and over hostile tariffs to the civilized markets of the U.S.A., Europe and the colonies. The firm did not export to Asia, which since the 1840s had provided the cotton industry with its largest foreign markets. Thus it did not need to acquire mills in the great producing centres of Oldham and Blackburn which were heavily dependent on the Eastern trade. Rylands did not believe in middlemen but favoured the establishment of direct contact between producer and consumer. He replied to a boycott imposed by the London wholesale colonial houses of all English manufacturers and merchants serving colonial drapers by immediately sending his travellers to the overseas colonies.[100] Thus he entered a rapidly expanding trade and imitated the example of the home-trade houses of Glasgow which had made the colonial trade into the backbone of their business. The high quality of the firm's goods was recognized by the award of medals at exhibitions held at Adelaide in 1887, at Brussels and Melbourne in 1888 and at Paris in 1889. Its export trade would probably have been even greater if foreign states had followed Britain's example in adopting free trade.

Always conscious of the importance of transport costs, Rylands gave more support than any other cotton manufacturer to the scheme for a Manchester Ship Canal which matured during the recession of 1882. He attended the historic meeting called by the engineer Daniel Adamson on 27 June 1882 to consider the project, became a member of the provisional committee and subscribed to the two guarantee funds required by the projectors. He subscribed £10,000 with the promise of another £50,000 to the Manchester Ship Canal Company which was established in 1886.[101] Thus he took up 6,000 shares or sixfold the number applied for by the C.W.S.[102] His contribution was of vital importance in so far as it was made during the critical period when the fate of the whole venture hung in the balance. The immense project promised indeed to save him £5,000 per annum,[103] or 2 per cent on the £250,000 of cotton which his firm imported every year, as well as to enhance the freehold value of the extensive Longford estate in Stretford. Rylands was, however, inspired as much by a sense of public interest as by a desire for private profit since Manchester merchants in general abstained from risking their capital in an uneconomic venture which

[100] *Manchester City News*, 15 Dec. 1888, 5iv.

[101] B.T. Leech, *History of the Manchester ship canal* (Manchester: Sherratt, 1907), i, 194; ii, 6, 7, 46.

[102] Greater Manchester Record Office, Archives of the Manchester Ship Canal Company, Minutes of the Board of Directors, i, 33, 2 Oct. 1885.

[103] *Textile Manufacturer*, Aug. 1890, 395.

paid no dividends on its ordinary shares for twenty-two long years after its completion in 1894.[104]

Rylands & Sons developed its own *esprit de corps* as its fortunes prospered. It provided a range of social facilities and fostered the establishment of employee associations such as benevolent societies, thrift funds, recreational clubs, brass and string bands, orchestras and dramatic societies. It maintained the morale of its employees simply by its success and by its provision of a job for life. Inevitably the firm benefited by the competition for employment in order to recruit the best commercial talent. It served as a great training-school in business method for the founders of other firms. Thus Richard Haworth (1820–83)[105] began his career as a book-keeper at the Ainsworth mill in 1839–43 before he became an independent manufacturer in Salford and built up the fourth largest firm in the cotton industry after those of Rylands, Horrockses and Tootal. George Booth (1807–86)[106] was employed by the firm for twenty-four years from 1829 until 1853 and then established the merchant firm of George and Hugh Booth (1853–72), becoming a member of the Manchester City Council in 1862, a J.P. in 1872 and an alderman in 1879. John Rhodes (1817–95)[107] was an employee from 1833 until 1868 and then became from 1868 to 1889 the head of Rhodes Brothers, merchants and manufacturers. During twenty-seven months at the Dacca Mills in 1868–71 W.F.M. Weston (1851–1937)[108] learned the necessity for methodical organization before he established his own yarn agency.

Even more important for the future of the firm were those businessmen trained by Rylands who remained with the firm. The death of his son and heir was a profound personal tragedy for John Rylands but it opened up for seventy years the full extent of an internal career to merit, irrespective of family connections. The opportunities for social mobility so offered were shown in the careers of many employees, including not least James Horrocks, Reuben Spencer and William Gregson. Spencer became a partner in the firm in 1867 and a director in 1873 and the main driving force in its expansion thereafter. He played an important role in the corporate life of the concern, wherein he helped to found in 1864 during the Cotton Famine the Porters' and Packers' Benevolent Society. In 1875 he became the chairman of the Home Trade

104 D.A. Farnie, *The Manchester ship canal and the rise of the port of Manchester 1894–1975* (Manchester: University Press, 1980), 22.

105 W.B. Pope, *A memorial of Richard Haworth, Esq., J.P. of Manchester* (Manchester: Day, 1885, 63pp.).

106 *Manchester Guardian*, 3 July 1886, 9ii. R Spencer, *The home trade of Manchester* (1890), 151–4.

107 *Textile Manufacturer*, Dec. 1895, 453.

108 W.F.M. Weston-Webb, *The autobiography of a British yarn merchant* (Richards, 1929), 44–57.

Association established in 1841 and in 1878 the chairman of the Warehousemen and Clerks' Provident Association established in 1856: he also helped to found in 1883 the United Commercial Travellers' Association. He became a keen supporter of the Manchester Ship Canal,[109] establishing a share-subscription system for employees of the firm in 1887. He followed the example of his employer in declining political ambitions.

The best measure of the success of the firm is to be found not merely in its survival and expansion but also in its financial performance. During the sixteen years 1873–88 it made average annual profits on its immense capital of 3.6 per cent. It also built up a large reserve fund, which rose in amount from £8,774 in 1873 to £265,516 in 1888 and which was buttressed by a further reserve of £500,000 in uncalled share capital and by a concealed reserve in the site value of its properties in Manchester and in London. The reserve fund had to be raided on three occasions, in 1878, 1879 and 1881 in order to maintain the level of dividends. On the paid-up share capital of £1,500,000 the dividends paid over the sixteen years aggregated £1,273,547 or 85 per cent gross. They averaged 5.3 per cent per annum, being 10 per cent for four years (1873–76) but declining to 5.6 per cent for the next twelve years (1877–88) (Table 2). The bulk of the dividends accrued to John Rylands himself, as the largest shareholder. His income from the firm was further swollen by about one-half by the 5 per cent interest which he drew from his cash deposit with the company, a balance which more than doubled from £282,788 at the close of 1873 to £625,776 at the close of 1878. By using his profits to make all of his shares fully paid he identified his personal fortune more closely than ever with the firm which bore his name.

8. The external interests of John Rylands, 1870–88, especially as a philanthropist

John Rylands has been harshly criticized for being interested only in the making of money.[110] He has been belittled as a tight-fisted millowner who made a fortune at the expense of his employees by paying low wages. Such criticisms need to be set in historical perspective. First, making a fortune in the cotton industry was never easy, particularly during the era when John Rylands flourished and competition became more intense than ever. The money made by John Rylands was certainly not made at the expense of his workforce. His abiding interest remained the creation of a great and viable business. In fulfilling that aim he performed a considerable

---

[109] R. Spencer, *The home trade of Manchester* (1890), 58–63; idem, *To young men going out into life* (Manchester: Heywood, 1891), 257–89; idem, *History of Lancashire* (1897), 24–34, 50–72.

[110] Weston-Webb, *Autobiography* (1929), 61.

social service by giving secure employment for so long to so many (Table 1). Secondly, John Rylands made a fortune simply by producing goods of quality and by selling them cheaply. In consequence the economic world beat a path to the doors of his warehouse and thrust money into his hands in exchange for his wares. In other words he made his money in free, fair and open competition with other merchants. Thus he conferred substantial benefits upon the consuming public, both working-class and middle-class. Thirdly, the profit-ratio of his firm remained consistently low (Table 2): its high returns were generated by a swelling turnover. The mere rational refutation of such criticisms will not however dispose of them. They will recur because they stem from the deepest well-springs of human motives: they originate in invincible ignorance, in ingrained envy and in indestructible prejudice, especially a bias against the making of money, a pursuit which has been one of the most popular national pastimes for at least the past millenium. No amount of countervailing evidence will ever serve to convince the narrow-minded holders of such negative views, who seem to personify what Goethe termed 'the Spirit, which always denies'.

John Rylands became one of the most notable philanthropists of the age, proving that he knew how to use money as well as how to make it. His mode of life was not that of an ascetic. Dr Andrew Fairbairn said of him in 1899: 'The character we associate with the Puritan of the seventeenth century had in him its modern embodiment'.[111] That judgement, made on the occasion of the inauguration of the John Rylands Library, may need to be set in perspective. John Rylands remained a Puritan with a difference. He loved a game of chess, billiards, bowls or croquet. He adorned his home with books, water-colours, engravings and statues sculpted in bronze or marble. He appreciated a fine wine and stocked the cellars at Longford Hall judiciously. He put his ample income to good use. Recognizing that he would pass through the world but once, he did not defer his benefactions until his death. In maturity his interests remained strongly religious and philanthropic. At the age of seventy he was inspired by the apparently apocalyptic entry of Italian troops in 1870 into the capital of the papal monarchy. His interest in the evangelization of Italy deepened: he visited the country, learned the language and established an orphanage in the Trastevere district of Rome. As 'a New Testament man – pure and simple'[112] he had already sponsored the publication in 1867 of *Il*

---

[111] *Manchester Guardian*, 7 Oct. 1899, 7i.
[112] Local Studies Library of the Manchester Central Library, Newspaper Cuttings – Biography, s.v. Rylands, John, containing a letter by Charles Swallow to C.W. Sutton, dated 21 June 1877.

Nuovo Testamento. That work was followed in 1870 by *Le Nouveau Testament,* a reprint of the French translation by J.F. Ostervald. Both were private publications and were distributed independently of the British and Foreign Bible Society. Thereafter he turned his attention to the preparation of a second edition of his paragraph Bible. His liberal benefactions to the poor of Rome earned recognition, if not from the Pope, from the King of Italy, who in 1880 conferred on him the fifth class of an order of merit created in 1868, making him a Knight of the Order of the Crown of Italy.

In his philanthropic activity he was, as a strict economist, unsympathetic to small causes but he maintained a large number of pensioners and kept secret many of his largest benefactions. Remembering his own successive bereavements he made special provision not only for the orphan but also for the widow and for the aged poor. From 1875 he renewed his philanthropic activity. In that year he acquired a new London residence and he married, for the first time in a Congregational Chapel, Enriqueta Augustina Tennant, who had been the companion of Martha Rylands during her later years. He did not carry through his plan of 1876 to build a residential hall near the new buildings of Owens College for the Lancashire Independent College. That scheme was strongly supported by Cavendish but John Rylands changed his mind and severed his connection with the chapel. Instead he financed the construction in 1877 of a terrace of six cottages at Sunnyside in the grounds of Longford Park, to provide a home for aged gentlewomen. Increasingly he concentrated his charitable interests upon Stretford. Ainsworth, Gorton and Greenheys had been in succession the objects of his philanthropy: now it was to be the turn of Stretford. Wigan was dominated by the earls of Crawford and had been presented in 1878 with a free public library by another local cotton spinner, Thomas Taylor (1808–92). In Stretford however John Rylands had become a virtual lord of the manor to the Longford district. He could not of course rival the influence of the Trafford family and he had to co-exist with the Local Board of Health created in 1868. He almost trebled the size of his estate to seventy-nine acres by the successive purchase of some fifty-four separate properties (1856–76) for £65,712. By 1881 he was receiving a rental income of £3,500 per annum from 121 local tenants. He may have aspired to have his principal employees as the tenants of his estate: two directors, William Linnell and W.D. Gloyne, had the rents of their Stretford houses paid by the firm. His good works did include several local foundations. First, in 1878 he built a town hall for Stretford. The town hall itself cost £11,600 and was equipped with a gymnasium in the basement and a public hall on the first floor, furnished with an organ (for the local Sunday School), accommodation for 300 and a gallery to seat another sixty persons. Secondly, he established a free lending library, with 3,000 volumes, in 1883, and public baths, at a cost of £4,320, in 1886–87. Thirdly, in 1883, he established a coffee-house. In turn that foundation gave rise to the Longford Institute opened in 1886 with a bowling-green, a tennis-court and a children's playground. That institute was replicated in both Haven Street and Heapey. John Rylands did not, however, become the effective overlord of Stretford: even less did he become a leader of Manchester society.[113]

In 1882 John Rylands acquired a country seat in the village of Haven Street near Ryde. There he rented a pew in the Baptist Church at Ryde during the ministry of W.S. Davis (1839–94). There he established in 1886 another Longford Institute, endowing its library with 500 books.[114] During the closing years of his life his interest in hymns became greater than ever before. Originally John Rylands had seen in such compositions a distinctively Nonconformist contribution to congregational participation in worship. Increasingly he came to recognize in them the inner unity and hidden harmony of the Churches of Christ which could not find embodiment in their creed. His collection had risen by one half to number some 30,000 by 1864: it swelled further to 50,000 by 1885 and ultimately to 60,000, or to some 15 per cent of the 400,000 then in existence in English. The collection was 'peculiarly rich in the pious effusions of the old Calvinistic School, which are now seldom to be met with elsewhere'.[115] Its resources were drawn upon in the last two of his publications, undertaken with the aid of Dr S.G. Green. *Hymns of the Church Universal* (1886) was the most characteristic of all the publications of John Rylands while *Hymns for the young* (1887) was designed for use in Sunday Schools and especially for Stretford.

By 1886 John Rylands had acquired landed estates in England aggregating some 230 acres. He did not however become a member of the landed gentry and he never sought to imitate the tastes of the aristocracy, declining to keep horses or hounds or menservants. Thus he refused to follow the example set by Arkwright, Strutt, Peel, Bazley and Fielden in buying the social status conferred by landownership. The death of his son and heir would have made such a course of action pointless. The soil of England, which had been systematically enriched by vast capitals accumulated in trade, was denied one great prize. The Rylands fortune remained in liquid investments and could therefore be turned in the fullness of time to creative use.

---

[113] *Whitehall Review*, 31 Aug. 1882, 11, 'Provincial society. Manchester'.

[114] *Baptist Handbook*, 1895, 152, for W.S. Davis. *Isle of Wight County Press*, 7 Aug. 1886, 3; 15 Dec. 1888, 5.

[115] JRL., The Hymn Collection of John Rylands (1900, 34 vols), Preface.

9. The death of John Rylands, the creation of the John Rylands Library, and the achievements of Edward Gordon Duff as the first Librarian

This library is very near my heart, and when thinking or speaking about it I get sometimes carried away further than I intended.

JRL., Library Archives, Mrs E.A. Rylands to
William Linnell, 19 March 1891.

John Rylands slackened the pace of his activity in his eighties. He still controlled the firm until 1886–87 but he did not renew his subscription to the Manchester Royal Exchange after 1876 and he spoke little at shareholders' meetings after 1878, although he continued to preside over them. His health began to deteriorate from 1886 and worsened sharply during the summer of 1887. The board of directors became concerned about the decline in returns to capital and decided on 25 January 1887 to restrict any further increase in fixed capital. From 11 June 1887 the board began to hold regular weekly meetings and assumed effective control of the firm. The directors began to make important changes in business policy. They introduced regular monthly summaries of profit and loss and used those statistics as the basis for remedial action. From 1888 they began to sell off loss-making mills, together with unprofitable ancillary properties. They authorized expenditure upon publicity, in the first instance through a twenty-page brochure. From 1888 they introduced regular July sales in order to even out seasonal fluctuations in demand. They also began to conclude price-fixing agreements with some of their competitors.

During his own lifetime John Rylands seems to have remained relatively unknown outside Lancashire and Cheshire. On 6 December 1888 he took, for the last time, a drive in the winter sunshine. On 11 December, at the age of eighty-seven, he died. The death of the greatest merchant of the age passed almost unnoticed in London.[116] The funeral was not attended by any official representative of the Manchester City Council. Both directors and shareholders paid solemn tribute to his character, to 'his repeated acts of kindness to each of us in the different spheres we have filled

---

[116] *The Times*, 12 Dec. 1888. 9vi. The fullest obituaries are to be found in the *Manchester Examiner*, 12 Dec. 1888, 5v–vii and in the *Manchester City News*, 15 Dec. 1888, 5ii–v. There are shorter notices in: *Manchester Guardian*, 12 Dec. 1888, 8iii–iv; *Manchester Courier*, 12 Dec. 1888, 8vii–viii; *Manchester Weekly Times*, 15 Dec. 1888, 2v–vi; *Wigan Observer*, 12 Dec. 1888, 5i; *Gorton, Openshaw and Bradford Reporter*, 15 Dec. 1888, 6iv; *Cotton Factory Times*, 14 Dec. 1888, 7iii–iv; *Textile Manufacturer*, 15 Dec. 1888, 562–3. The *St Helens Chronicle*, 8 March 1889, includes a critical note on the lack of any bequest to his native town, a reference I owe to Mrs Diana K. Jones. No reference to any article on John Rylands appears in W.I. Fletcher (ed.), *Poole's Index to Periodical Literature, Second Supplement 1887–1892* (Kegan Paul, 1893).

at his side for these many years'[117] and to his ability. The hard-headed William Carnelley paid a heart-felt tribute to 'our beloved' and 'our dear Governor', setting the example which was followed by the hard-headed shareholders. 'This meeting desires to place on record its high appreciation of the great business capacity, the unwearied diligence, the fine courtesy, the inflexible firmness, the wise sagacity, the high integrity, the pure sincerity and the unostentatious charity which being united to a character of high moral tone served to endear him to all who were brought into any kind of relation with him'.[118] His personal estate of £2,574,922 represented the largest fortune left by any cotton manufacturer down to that date. It furnished a striking contrast to the estates of £26,829 left by his father in 1847, of £90,000 left by his brother Joseph in 1853 and of £5,000 left by his brother Richard in 1863. In his will John Rylands bequeathed 19,000 shares in his firm valued at £377,500 to three main groups of legatees, £163,000 to religious, educational and charitable institutions, £128,000 to named directors and employees of the firm, and £86,500 to relatives and friends. His support of churches, chapels and schools was continued by the firm as a matter of course whilst his other charitable interests were cared for by his widow. Enriqueta Augustina Rylands became his chief legatee and sole executor. As such she became the chief shareholder in the two leading business firms of Manchester. She inherited 43,400 shares in the firm (98 per cent of which were fully paid) worth £863,820, together with the 6,000 shares in the Manchester Ship Canal Company. The growth in the market value of the shares in Rylands & Sons Ltd more than compensated for the decline in value of the shares of the Manchester Ship Canal Company. Mrs Rylands determined to strengthen the firm built up by her late husband. His legacies in shares strengthened the *esprit de corps* within the firm and increased the number of shareholders to 600 but reduced the shareholding of Mrs Rylands from 61 per cent to 44 per cent. For twenty years she served as a superb steward to her husband's fortune. When she died in 1908 she left an estate of £3,448,692 including £908,000 in shares in Rylands & Sons Ltd as well as £416,201 in the stock of home railways. Her charitable benefactions totalled £473,000, surpassing those of her husband.

Mrs Rylands determined to commemorate her late husband in the most fitting manner. She decided in 1889 to create a great library as the most suitable of all memorials. She also encouraged Dr Samuel G. Green to compose a memoir for private circulation.

---

[117] JRL., Archives of Rylands & Sons Ltd, Minutes of the Board of Directors, i, 131, 15 Dec. 1888, letter of the directors to Mrs Rylands.
[118] Idem., General Meetings Minute Book, 115, 8 Feb. 1889.

She employed his son, Arnold Green (1860–1907) as her exclusive and confidential agent in the purchase of works for the new library. She arranged for the construction of the Rylands Memorial which was completed in 1892 above the tomb in Southern Cemetery. In 1894 she presented the Rylands Cricket Challenge Shield to the Manchester Company of the Boys' Brigade. She was well aware of the distinctive needs of both the Nonconformist communities and of Manchester. The Nonconformists had thrived during an era of intolerance: they began to decline with the abolition of discriminatory legislation between 1828 and 1900. The number of Nonconformists reached an absolute peak during the year 1906, especially for Methodists and Baptists, with Congregationalists peaking in 1907. The picture changes somewhat when one estimates the proportion of the population professing adherence to different faiths. Dissent in general, when measured by the issue of certificates to places of worship, had reached a peak during the 1820s after some thirty years of expansion. Rated by its proportion of the population, it peaked eighty years later in 1906. Within the spectrum of Nonconformity Methodists registered their peak proportion of the population in 1841, Congregationalists in 1851 but Baptists only in 1906.[119] For too long the Nonconformist communities had dwelled in disdainful isolation. 'It can hardly be denied that Nonconformity has not the weight with the educated classes of the country which it has with the commercial classes. It fills but a small place in public life. Some of its greatest leaders are comparatively unknown. Its special literature wants, as a rule, the *cachet* of a refined scholarship and a delicate style. Its social importance is vastly inferior to its political importance. Its intellectual influence is not at all adequate to its real intellectual force'.[120] Mrs Rylands sought to remedy that imbalance and to create an immense library of theology for the Nonconformist world of northern England, so carrying further the revival which had begun therein during the 1890s and culminated in the great Nonconformist renaissance of 1901–06. She decided to house that library in her own adopted city of Manchester. She was well aware of the reputation of the town as the home of the philistine. She was familiar with its cultural deficiencies and aware that Owens College could not alleviate those shortcomings.

Mrs Rylands began to change her plans when in 1892 she bought the library of Earl Spencer at Althorp for £210,000. That

[119] R. Currie, A. Gilbert, L. Horsley, *Churches and churchgoers: patterns of church growth in the British Isles since 1700* (Oxford: Clarendon Press, 1977), 25, 65, 148, 150.
[120] *Methodist Times*, i:24 (11 June 1885), 370, 'Nonconformity at Oxford' by Edwin Hatch (1835–89) reader in ecclesiastical history and Bampton lecturer for 1880 in the University of Oxford. J.C.G. Binfield, *So down to prayers: studies in English nonconformity, 1780–1920* (Dent, 1977).

Figure 17: Enriqueta Augustina Rylands and Stephen Joseph Tennant, *c.* 1890
Stephen Tennant (1843–1914) was the twin brother of the third Mrs Rylands. He entered the employ of the firm after his sister's marriage and looked after its shipping interests, especially to America. The eldest of his three sons, Stephen Leonard Tennant, became an architect and was engaged upon the John Rylands Library in the 1890s. The father became from 1899 a trustee and honorary treasurer of that library as well as a director of the firm from 1901.

(John Rylands Library, Library Archives, Newspaper Cuttings, i, 154, The Gentlewoman, 15 Feb. 1908, a photograph taken by Rose H. Durrant of Torquay; P.L. Tennant, Esq.)

Figure 18: Group of Statues in the Foyer of the John Rylands Library, 1993, symbolizing Science, Theology and Art.

The group represents Theology in the centre, clasping the volume of Holy Writ, and directing Science, depicted as an aged man holding a globe, absorbed in study and discovery; while Art, in the form of a youthful metal-worker shaping a chalice, turns aside to listen. The thought conveyed is that Science and Art alike derive their highest impulses and perform their noblest achievements, only as they discern their consummation in Religion. [H. Guppy], The John Rylands Library. Memorial of the Inauguration. Presented by Mrs Rylands, 7 October, 1899 (Blades, 1899), 11.

(John Rylands Library)

acquisition entailed a whole series of changes at Longford Hall, including the sacrifice of John Rylands's own personal library as a necessary prelude to the creation of the greater John Rylands Library. It is a reasonable assumption that the dispersal of that collection was an indirect result of the purchase in 1892 of the Althorp Library. Some 2,000 of the 43,000 volumes were left behind at Althorp, from whence others seem to have been stolen.[121] The arrival however of some 600 cases at Longford Hall, added to the 10–15,000 volumes already acquired for the memorial library created a host of problems, many of which Mrs Rylands had not apparently foreseen. The primary need was to preserve the security of one of the most valuable private libraries in the world. To that end Mrs Rylands implemented certain precautionary measures. The most valuable works were deposited in the strong room in the cellar, which was modelled on the strong room in the basement of the firm's Manchester warehouse and which in turn supplied the model for the strong room in the basement of the new library being erected on Deansgate. Other works were distributed in bookcases or on the new shelves which were hastily installed from September 1892 but which proved to be thoroughly unsatisfactory. 'I paid what I consider a high price for the work and we have not a shelf which does not bend like a bow in the centre'.[122] Under such pressure on the available space the library of John Rylands was broken up, in order to make room for the new acquisitions. Many volumes were sold but not apparently by auction, since no sale catalogue has survived. Others were sent as gifts to various destinations such as Milton College,[123] the Rylands Book Depository in Stretford Town Hall, or the Rylands Home and Orphanage.[124] Mrs Rylands replaced the gas lighting at Longford Hall by electric lighting in 1892–93 in order to avoid any damage to the books. She extended the provision of electric light to the John Rylands Library itself in 1894, in an innovation which had not been planned in 1889. Longford Hall's water supply was enlarged so as to increase the volume which would be available in case of fire. Two night watchmen were hired to patrol the grounds of the park. Above all, Mrs Rylands had to insure the collection against any possible loss and she had to appoint a librarian in order to catalogue it, for the

121 JRL., Library Archives, Mrs E.A. Rylands to William Linnell, 6 Dec. 1893.

122 JRL., Mrs E.A. Rylands to Basil Champneys, 24 Feb. 1893.

123 A school at Ullesthorpe to the south of Leicester which was attended by Arthur Forbes, her adopted son.

124 The Rylands Home and Orphanage is referred to variously in the Library Catalogue of 1881 as 'R.H.', or as 'Rylands Home' or as 'Greenhill Street'. The home was sold by Mrs Rylands in 1894. The building was used in 1895 by the Hulme Social Club and in 1899 by the Lancashire College Settlement. *Manchester Faces and Places*, xi (3 March 1900), 37.

purpose of insurance. That task was undertaken from 1893 by Edward Gordon Duff (1863–1924).[125]

Mrs Rylands had spent four years in creating a library with the help of her own advisers but without the guidance of any professional librarian. Her relations with Duff did not become close and she did not admit him to the intimate circle of her court. The two persons had little in common apart from their Scots descent and their Nonconformity. Duff's preference for discourse with his intellectual peers made him reluctant to seek counsel from Mrs Rylands or from her advisers. He did achieve some early measure of success. He suggested the use of a bookplate, which was duly designed, approved and printed in 1894. He also prevented Mrs Rylands from wasting money on inappropriate shelving for the book cases. Duff however worked out his own plans for those cases 'as usual, with the help and advice of friends'.[126] A preliminary catalogue of the library was compiled, presumably for purposes of insurance. The list of early printed books clearly revealed the limits of Duff's bibliographical interests and was printed by J.E. Cornish (1831–1903) of Manchester. Mrs Rylands's opinion of the *Catalogue of books in the John Rylands Library, Manchester, printed in England, Scotland and Ireland and of books in English printed abroad to the end of the year 1640* (Manchester, Cornish, 1895, 147pp) remains unknown. What does seem certain however is that the stock of the catalogue printed in 1895 was not distributed until 1900.[127]

---

[125] For Duff see *The Library*, 5 (1924–25), 264–6 (Falconer Madan); *Library Association Record*, n.s. 2 (1924), 226–8 (S. Gibson); *Manchester Review*, 5 (Winter 1948), 177–9 (W.G. Fry); *Transactions of the Cambridge Bibliographical Society*, 9 (1990), 5, 409–33 (Arnold Hunt), the last reference being one I owe to Mr H. Horton. There is also a chapter on 'Duff and Proctor' in H.F. Stewart, *Francis Jenkinson, Fellow of Trinity College and University Librarian* (Cambridge University Press, 1926), 30–4.

[126] JRL., Library Archives, Mrs E.A. Rylands to W. Linnell, 12 March 1895.

[127] Three items of evidence testify to the lapse of five years. First, the acquisition of both works by the Manchester Central Library during the year 1900. The 1899 Catalogue was accessioned on 24 Jan. 1900 and the 1895 Catalogue ten months later, on 12 Nov. 1900, i.e. after Duff's resignation. Manchester Public Free Library, Reference Department, Register of Accessions, 23 Nov. 1898–24 Nov. 1900, 118, 198. A similar gap of ten months (and 720 items) occurs in the Owens College Library, Register of Additions, 4 (1892–1901) between the two dates of 29 Jan. 1900 (for the 1899 Catalogue) and 20 Nov. 1900 (for the 1895 Catalogue). The Register of Accessions of the John Rylands Library 1 (1900–1906) contains no entry for either catalogue. Secondly, the absence of any recorded reference in 1895 to the 1895 Catalogue in registers of accessions, in catalogues of publications or in reviews of books published. Thirdly, the coincidence of reviews of both catalogues in the year 1900, indicating that the two catalogues had been issued together. The three-volume catalogue was sent alone in April 1900 for review to *The Times* and the *Daily Chronicle*. Both catalogues were however, sent to at least five other journals, *The Spectator*, the *Scotsman*, the *Manchester Courier*, the *Athenaeum* and the *Manchester Guardian*. There they were reviewed in tandem and the catalogue of early printed books to 1640 was explicitly mentioned as being 'also issued' (*Manchester Courier*, 2 May 1900). The *Manchester Guardian* of 29 Aug. 1900 was emphatic. 'For the second of the two books sent to us . . . we have nothing but praise'. The review in *The Spectator* for 14 April 1900 of the 'four volume' catalogue noted that 'the early English books . . . have a volume to themselves'. There remains a presumption that certain reviewers knew the reason for the delay since none commented upon the issue in 1900 of a work bearing an 1895 imprint.

The delay of five years in publication must have dealt a severe blow to Duff. Thereafter Mrs Rylands decided to appoint a separate and superior Chief Librarian for the John Rylands Library.[128] The qualifications identified as appropriate in her new functionary seem to represent the opposite of Duff's own talents. The Chief Librarian was to possess a thorough knowledge of general literature and mainly of theology. He would be styled 'President' while Duff would remain as Keeper of Early Printed Books.[129] In effect his fate had already been decided, probably during the year 1895.

Mrs Rylands arranged through Duff for the sale in 1896 of 305 lots of 'Rylands duplicates'.[130] She also began to build up her own personal library, compiling in 1896 a list of those books which she wished to keep out of the John Rylands Library. By the close of 1896 Duff had completed the preparation of the main catalogue, whose pages when printed extended to fourteenfold the number in the 1895 Catalogue.[131] In discussion Duff had failed to secure his own way upon such details as the placing of the Christian name of the author in brackets. Above all, he was frustrated in his wish to add two more catalogues, a subject index and sectional catalogues relating to special portions of the library.[132] That proposal was vetoed, perhaps because Mrs Rylands had decided that she did not wish to prolong his employment. Mrs Rylands then despatched confidential instructions to the printers, requesting them to inform her if they were 'not fully and promptly furnished with copy and regular returns of proof'.[133] In the event the catalogue, prepared under such unpropitious conditions, took twice as long to print as had been expected and was not completed in time for the inauguration of the library on 6 October 1899.[134]

[128] JRL., Library Archives, Mrs Rylands to W. Linnell, 13 April 1896.

[129] JRL., Library Archives, Mrs Rylands, Draft Regulations for the John Rylands Library, 1899.

[130] JRL., *Catalogue of valuable books and manuscripts selected from the library of a gentleman . . . also another property, containing county histories and topographical works, chiefly on large paper; books of prints; complutensian polyglott and other rare Bibles and Testaments; Old English chronicles, & cc., & c. which will be sold by auction by Messrs, Sotheby, Wilkinson & Hodge . . . on Friday, 27th of November 1896* (Dryden Press, 1896, 58pp.), listing on 40–58 the items sold for £1615.

[131] *Catalogue of the printed books and manuscripts in the John Rylands Library, Manchester*, 3 vols (Manchester: Cornish, 1899).

[132] JRL., Library Archives, W. Linnell to E.G. Duff, 12 March 1897, in the Champneys Letters, iii, 107–8; E.G. Duff to W. Linnell, 16 March 1897, in volume inscribed 'A8', 5–6.

[133] JRL., Library Archives, W. Linnell to J.& A. Constable of Edinburgh, 31 May 1897, in Vol. 'A8', p.20. Presumably Constable disclosed the full text to Duff who transcribed the letter in the volume 'A8' which he may have begun to keep in 1897 as some form of insurance policy.

[134] D.A. Farnie, 'Enriqueta Augustina Rylands (1843–1908), founder of the John Rylands Library', *Bulletin of the John Rylands Library of the University of Manchester*, 71: 2 (Summer 1989), 16–32. On the inauguration ceremonies see the *Manchester Guardian*, 5 Aug. 1899, 7vii; 7 Oct., 6–7, 9iii–iv; *Manchester Courier*, 6 Oct. 1899, 10ii–iv, 7 Oct., 6iii, 9i–vi; *Manchester City News*, 7 Oct. 1899, 2iii, 5iii–v; *Manchester Faces and Places*, xi: 3, March 1900, 35–41; Basil Champneys, 'The John Rylands Library, Manchester', *Journal of the Royal Institute of British Architects*, 27 Jan. 1900, 101–14; Cecil Stewart, *The stones of Manchester* (Arnold, 1956), 123–7.

In April 1899 Mrs Rylands appointed a Wesleyan, Henry Guppy, as Joint Librarian with Duff, dealing another heavy blow to his pride. Then a vicious review of the three-volume catalogue appeared in the leading paper of the day. The anonymous notice criticized the work for its 'bald entries' and for the idiosyncrasies of the compiler. 'It is deeply to be regretted that this catalogue is only a mere list and of very little value to the bibliographical student'.[135] Duff had also made enemies in Manchester as well as in London. He became convinced that he had been, ever since the inauguration, the object of a campaign of systematic harassment conducted by two of the library's new trustees. Both William Carnelley and William Linnell were senior directors of Rylands & Sons Ltd. Carnelley was chairman of the firm in 1900 while Linnell was chairman of the board of governors of the library. Together they disturbed Duff deeply by their ignorance and by their perpetual and intolerable interference, 'in every possible way', in day to day administration. Presumably their actions had been sanctioned by Mrs Rylands. Duff could secure no support from the other trustees or governors and decided to surrender his office. He gave notice of his intention to resign with effect from 15 October 1900, first verbally and then by formal letter. The resignation created consternation in the literary world of Lancashire but was immediately accepted by Carnelley and Linnell, who did not even formally consult the board of governors. For Mrs Rylands the year 1900 proved to be a most unfortunate one: it began with the disinheriting of her own adopted daughter, Maria, and it closed with the loss of the most distinguished bibliographer ever to serve the John Rylands Library. In retrospect what may seem remarkable is not that Duff resigned but that he laboured for seven long years under such conditions. 'Duff declares that nothing would induce him to go through what he has done since the place was opened'.[136] His own memorial is embodied in the material equipment and organization of the John Rylands Library and in the great three-volume catalogue of 1899.

In 1889 Mrs Rylands had provided for a manuscript room as an essential feature of the new library. It was however twelve years later that she added to the volumes of the Althorp Library an invaluable collection of manuscripts. She bought the Crawford Manuscripts for £155,000 in 1901 but was so impressed by their beauty that she retained them at Longford Hall, taking out a special

[135] *The Times*, 23 April 1900.
[136] National Library of Scotland, Edinburgh, Department of Manuscripts, Bibliotheca Lindesiana Letters, Acc.9769, J.P. Edmond to Ludovic Lindsay, 25th earl of Crawford, 8 September 1900, a reference for which I remain indebted to Mr Nicolas Barker. See also N. Barker, *Bibliotheca Lindesiana* (Quaritch, 1978), 332, quoting the letter by J.P. Edmond to the Earl of Crawford, 11 June 1896, on the visit paid by Carnelley and Linnell to Haigh Hall.

insurance policy on them on 7 May 1903. Only as her health continued to deteriorate[137] did she decide to release them. A special conference between Mrs Rylands and the governors on 17 October 1903 arranged for their transfer, which began in Novmber 1903 and January 1904. Thus the library acquired its second great collection and became a leading repository of manuscripts.

After the death of Mrs Rylands in 1908 two libraries were sold off. The library of 325 volumes at Queen's Gate, Kensington, was sold in 1908, although three lots comprising 25 paragraph Bibles, 130 Italian New Testaments and 140 French New Testaments were withdrawn from the sale. In 1910 Mrs Rylands's own library of 183 lots of 'valuable modern books' was sold.[138] The 5,000 volumes remaining at Longford Hall were however bequeathed to the John Rylands Library. Presumably those volumes comprised those which had been reserved in 1896: they included illuminated manuscripts as well as fine art works, works descriptive of the great art galleries, editions de luxe of modern literature, a collection of works printed on vellum, many in fine bindings by master binders, a large collection of autograph letters and historical documents including the collection formed by the Revd Dr Thomas Raffles of Liverpool and a fine set of the four folios of Shakespeare. Those works were duly accessioned during the year 1909 and included a number of books from the personal library of John Rylands himself.[139]

In the John Rylands Library Mrs Rylands invested altogether a sum of about a million pounds. The greater library resembled the lesser one in its original organization around the broad theme of religion. Dr Andrew Fairbairn, Principal of Mansfield College, Oxford, reaffirmed the purpose of the donor as the wish to create an enduring memorial to an unassuming Manchester man, who had been 'a modest merchant, a dutiful citizen and a humble lover of letters.' The library was designed 'to incorporate the mind of the man it commemorates, and [to] illustrate his character and its sources as they appeared to the person who knew him best'. 'The great fundamental, the essential character of the library, is that it is Biblical and theological, a great means for educating men in Scriptural knowledge'.[140] In the foyer a group of statues, placed in

---

[137] Mrs Rylands made at least eight tours of Europe between 1890 and 1900. There is no record of her travelling abroad after 1900. The worsening of her health is reflected in her purchase of villas, first in the spa town of Buxton in 1899 and then in Torquay in 1905. To the latter villa she had three cases of books shipped from the library in 1906.

[138] JRL., *Catalogue of the library of J. Gardiner Muir . . . also valuable modern books the property of a lady deceased, including the Kelmscott Chaucer, on vellum, and other productions of the Kelmscott Press. . . and other properties which will be sold by auction by Messrs. Sotheby, Wilkinson & Hodge on Tuesday, 21st June 1910, and two following days* (Dryden Press, 1910, 82pp.). *The Times*, 24 June 1910, 8iii, records that the total sale raised £1,960.

[139] JRL., Register of Accessions, 2 (1909), 266–89 lists at least 126 volumes from John Rylands's own library apart from the 182 volumes of his hymn books.

[140] *Manchester Guardian*, 7 Oct. 1899, 7i.

position in February 1898, symbolized the superiority of Theology to both Science and Art (Fig. 18). The group of three figures embodied the founder's own idea of the library's essential function. Mrs Rylands wished to make the group the central feature of the foyer. She insisted that the figures should stand out boldly from the wall and should not be cramped up in niches. In 1893 she considered, in a letter written to William Linnell on 8 March, whether the central statue of Religion should be seated, with 'the shield of faith' and 'an *open* Bible'. In 1895 she thought the group might most appropriately be surrounded by the coats of arms of the four cities of Manchester, Salford, Wigan and London. She abandoned both of those ideas but remained firm in her commitment to boldness of treatment of the group. She would not accept a proposal by the architect to moderate the impact of the central figure. Basil Champneys thought that a six foot female would have the effect of dwarfing the interior of the vestibule. He favoured a height of 4'6"–5': in the event the height became 5'4". John Cassidy (1860–1939) took three full years to complete the sculpture in red shauk stone. The finished work embodied in full the vision of Mrs Rylands. The group remains the most inspiring work of statuary in the whole building. It impresses visitors powerfully with a sense of other-worldly values and is reputed to have been sometimes mistaken for a statue of the Virgin Mary, an interpretation which would have dismayed Mrs Rylands.

The inauguration of the library helped to usher in a new era in the cultural history of Manchester. That era deserves its own name. If one divides the literary history of Manchester since the sixteenth century into four distinct phases, each of those eras may reasonably be associated with the particular name of a local luminary, such as Humphrey Chetham, John Byrom, Elizabeth Gaskell and finally, John Rylands.[141] Paradoxically each of those notables was associated with the religious life as well as with the literary history of the city. Thus the John Rylands Library was not inappropriately housed within a building which could be described as 'the real Manchester Cathedral. . . the Cathedral of today in Deansgate'.[142]

10. The firm at its apogee during the era of Spencer and Carnelley, 1887–1920

In the year after the death of John Rylands the firm's profits were larger than ever before. The board of directors was too conservative, however, to respond effectively to changes in the world of business.

---

[141] H.M. McKechnie, (ed.) *Manchester in 1915* (Manchester University Press, 1915), 92, 'The literature, drama, and music'. Allan Monkhouse, 'Literary associations: some Manchester books and bookmen', *Manchester Guardian Civic Week Number*, 2 Oct., 1926, 25.
[142] E.A. Parry, *What the judge saw, being twenty five years in Manchester* (Smith, 1912), 313.

In 1888 the four senior directors were on average sixty-six and a half years old and had each served the firm for some forty-three years. Since the 1870s great changes had been taking place in the structure of the textile trade, changes which increased the intensity of competition and worked to the firm's disadvantage. First, the home trade in clothing remained permanently stagnant and failed to increase its share of consumers' expenditure. Secondly, the traditional drapery trade, the corner-stone of the firm's business, began a long-term process of decline under the influence of inter-related changes in the whole structure of business. Those changes centred around the rise of the ready-made clothing industry, the growth of direct trade between clothing manufacturers and new major retailers, the spread of multiple-branch tailors and the entry of the C.W.S. from 1874 into the drapery trade. That transformation eroded the firm's connections with its traditional clientele and reduced progressively the demand for fustian. By 1887 at the latest Rylands & Sons were well aware of the threat. The firm could have met the challenge only by transforming its marketing strategy and its business structure. Such a transformation it failed to effect. Thirdly, the growing importance of fashion in the market place favoured light calicoes and new designs rather than the firm's traditional staples. New fabrics such as sateens, linenette and grandrilles and new finishes such as those imparted to mercerized and schreinered cloth came increasingly into favour. Rylands & Sons began to face competition from new centres of low-cost production in such staples as thread, shirtings, sateens, printers, flannelette, wadding and oil cloth. Fourthly, the Manchester trade faced increased competition from the merchant houses of London, Leicester and Nottingham. That competition used new commercial tactics such as the grant of longer credit terms and the payment of carriage costs. Thus London expanded its wholesale textile trade at the expense of Manchester and even increased its financial influence within Lancashire itself.

In the changed conditions of business Rylands & Sons was burdened by the declining productivity of labour in it mills[143] That trend was of the gravest import because it coincided with the growing loss of appetite amongst consumers for its own products. The firm faced a bitter conflict between its mercantile and its manufacturing interests. By 1888 the bulk of its textile sales were sales of outside makes, only 33 per cent being of its own products. Even in the basic trade in grey cloth only 39 per cent of sales were of its own manufacture. Similar competition was experienced in the trade in bleached cloth and in dyed goods. Most of its own goods had to be sold off at cost price and sometimes even at a loss.[144] The

---

[143] JRL., Archives of Rylands & Sons Ltd, Minutes of the Board of Directors, i, 82, 18 May 1888, J. Wright.
[144] Ibid., i, 139–140, 12 Jan. 1889, R. Spencer.

firm lost business despite a well-established reputation, a wide range of trade marks and the zealous protection of its brand names against all poachers. The returns on capital generated by the New High Street warehouses remained respectable but they represented ninefold the returns on capital generated by the mills. Aggregate returns on capital averaged only half of those generated by Horrockses during the years 1873–86, declining further in 1891–1900 to one-third of those of its great rival, which had surpassed it in loomage ever since the amalgamation of 1887.[145]

In response to the new conditions of trade a wide range of measures was introduced which were essentially adaptive rather than innovative. From 1889 directors' fees were first paid but were related to profits. For more effective administration departmental accounts were introduced in 1888 and sub-committees of the board were established in 1890. The firm began to withdraw resources from a number of unprofitable ancillary operations. In 1889 it decided not to expand its coal mining operations any further and in 1898 it closed down its Wigan collieries. It demolished Gorton Villa in 1890 and during the next fifteen years developed the grounds into a housing estate. In 1894 it closed the three mill schools at Gorton, Heapey and Wigan. In 1898 it closed the millwrights shop at Gorton. Expenditure upon publicity from 1887 and upon advertising from 1889 was sanctioned, even being extended to the advertising of Dacca calico. The firm sold off three mills in 1888–89 and three more in 1902, sharply reducing its labour force by 40 per cent (1889–1905) (Table 1). It abandoned the manufacture of thread after the creation of the Coats combine in 1896. It proved reluctant however to take more drastic decisions. It delayed the closure of its unprofitable Bolton mills for twelve years (1889–1902). It opened a large new wadding works at Gorton in 1894.[146] It also retained in production the works at both Gorton and Gidlow, despite their tendency to incur losses. 'The Mills must be kept going'.[147] The directors delayed the installation of sprinklers in the warehouses and the wholesale renewal of worn-out machinery in the mills. The chief engineer, F.W.C. Leeves, was appointed in order to succeed James Horrocks and spent seven years (1895–1902) vainly trying to persuade the board to renew its plant, finally resigning in disgust and frustration.[148]

More serious was the deliberate expansion of the firm's export business, a change in policy intended to compensate for the decline

---

[145] Lancashire Record Office, Preston, Records of Horrocks, Crewdson & Co Ltd listed at DDHs, Files 53 and 84.

[146] *Textile Manufacturer*, May 1894, 236.

[147] JRL., Archives of Rylands & Sons Ltd, Minutes of the Board of Directors, iv, 376, 16 June 1906.

[148] Ibid., iv, 71, 14 June 1902.

of trade with Europe, especially Italy, but involving great risks. Thus it entered the Australian trade during the boom year of 1891 and the South American trade on a larger scale from 1897.[149] It also began to import directly from Japan after the establishment in 1896 of the first Japanese steamship line to Europe.[150] The board did however reject ambitious proposals by Spencer, in 1891, to establish a branch works in the U.S.A. and in 1892 to develop trade with India. Indeed it withdrew from trade with the U.S.A. after 1900, with China and Singapore after 1903, and with South America after 1914, whilst still professing its interests to be 'world-wide'. The firm also began to modify its tradition of sturdy independence. From 1890 it began to join trade associations, depriving it of control from 1902 over its own wages policy and culminating in its accession in 1909 to the Manchester Cotton Spinners' Association. It also extended the network of price-fixing agreements with competitors. From 1891 it embarked upon a deliberate policy of investing capital outside the firm, beginning with first-class home railways and consols. By 1906 its outside investments equalled half of its paid-up share capital. Ominous portents began to appear upon the horizon. In 1907 it was forced to close down the first of forty-five departments, that for Stationery. In 1911 it gained at Turin its last award at an international exhibition.

What the firm really lacked after 1888 was a 'governor' of the calibre of John Rylands. The directors themselves recognized the magnitude of their loss. No other 'governor' of the company was ever appointed. The chairmanship of the board was placed in commission and devolved in rotation during the twelve years after 1888 upon three different directors, Spencer, Carnelley and Horrocks. James Horrocks (1832–1895) began his working life as a spinner at Ainsworth and became the director in charge of the manufacturing branch of the firm:[151] he served as chairman only once in 1894, during the last year of his life. Spencer enjoyed six terms of office (1889, 1892, 1893, 1896, 1897, 1899) and Carnelley four terms (1890, 1891, 1895, 1898). Reuben Spencer and William Carnelley were both men of immense ability, which they passed on to their sons.[152] Both had been born in textile towns, although outside Lancashire, Spencer in Belper and Carnelley in Barnsley. Both were mercantile rather than industrial in their expertise and outlook. Both were raised in the Nonconformist

[149] W.H. Zimmern, 'Lancashire and Latin America', *Geography*, June 1943, 53–4.

[150] E. Deiss, *À travers l'Angleterre industrielle et commerciale (notes de voyage)* (Paris: Guillaumin, 1898), 176–9

[151] JRL., Archives of Rylands & Sons Ltd, General Meetings Minute Book, 199–200, 8 Feb. 1895, R. Spencer. *Manchester Guardian*, 15 Jan. 1895.

[152] Thomas Carnelley (1852–90), professor of Chemistry from 1879 at Sheffield, Dundee and Aberdeen. Sir Walter Baldwin Spencer (1860–1920), professor of Biology at Melbourne (1887–1919), created a KCMG in 1916.

tradition, Spencer as a Congregationalist and Carnelley as a Wesleyan. Both lacked however that positive genius for business which John Rylands had possessed. Both paid tribute in print to the supreme talents of their late governor.[153]

Reuben Spencer undertook a number of steps to enhance his position and to raise his profile, within the firm, the board of directors and the community.[154] He established the Rylands Memorial Club in April 1889 but twice failed to persuade Mrs Rylands to become its patron.[155] His relations with Mrs Rylands were never close. He approved her purchase of the Althorp Library in the most condescending manner as one 'which he had no doubt would ultimately be for the benefit of the people of Manchester. It would be pleasing to our old employees as it was bought with money they had helped to make'.[156] In 1890 he became an ex-officio director of the Manchester Chamber of Commerce as the chairman of the newly-established Home Trade Sectional Committee. In 1892 he became vice-president of the Ship Canal Shareholders' Association, urged the firm to make use of the Ship Canal in order to ship goods to London via Saltport, and suggested that it should hire a special steamer for the inaugural voyage along the new waterway on 1 January 1894. In 1895 he became a vice-president of the Manchester Chamber of Commerce. On the occasion of his own commercial jubilee in 1897 he described the house of Rylands & Sons in glowing terms. 'We are, I believe, today the greatest textile house in the world'.[157] He became a keen advocate of the creation of a Greater Manchester. Such an entity might incorporate into one municipality all the districts and population within a four-mile radius of the Royal Exchange and would form an administrative unity appropriate to 'the industrial metropolis of the world'.[158]

Under Spencer and Carnelley the firm reached the heights of its prosperity, as measured by the level of its dividends. Debentures were first issued in 1889, to Mrs Rylands. Massive reserves were built up in the form of the firm's under-valued land, buildings and plant and in its reserve of £500,000 of uncalled share-capital. The

[153] W. Carnelley (compiler), *The questions of the Bible arranged in the order of the books of Scripture* (London: Unwin, 1889, 370pp.), with a preface by Dr S.G. Green and a dedication to the memory of John Rylands 'in token of a friendship of nearly fifty years'. R. Spencer, *The home trade of Manchester* (London: Simpkin, 1890), dedicated to the memory of John Rylands as 'a noble example of business capacity'.

[154] R. Spencer, *The home trade of Manchester* (1890); idem, *To young men going out into life* (1891).

[155] JRL., Archives of Rylands & Sons Ltd, Minutes of the Board of Directors, i, 67, 18 Feb. 1888; 157, 23 March 1889. General Meetings Minute Book, 146, 9 Feb. 1891.

[156] Ibid., General Meetings Minute Book, 164, 8 Aug. 1892.

[157] R. Spencer, *History of Lancashire* (1897), 194.

[158] R. Spencer, *The home trade of Manchester* (1890), 33–44; idem, *History of Lancashire* (1897), 47.

Reserve Fund rose from £191,000 in 1886 to £500,000 in 1894. A new Insurance Fund trebled in amount from £79,500 in 1896 to £250,000 in 1907, so forming against the opposition of many shareholders a gross reserve of £750,000. That increase in reserves avoided the need for any further issue of debentures or for any calls on shareholders, and made the firm more independent of outside contingencies as well as increasingly able to control the level of its dividends. The firm also accepted loans in the form of payments made in advance of calls by its shareholders and paid 5 per cent interest thereon. Under Spencer the average profit-ratio rose from 3.6 per cent (1873–88) to 4.4 per cent (1889–1900) but the average dividend soared from 5.3 per cent to 12.5 per cent. That remarkable achievement was effected with only a single raid on the reserves, undertaken in 1897. As dividends increased the premium on the £15-paid shares rose eight-fold from £3 in 1890 and £5 in 1892 to £25 in 1897,[159] more than doubling their market-price.

William Carnelley became managing director in 1896 and chairman in 1901, after the deaths of Horrocks in 1895 and of Spencer in 1901. He came to be regarded as 'the father of the commercial world in Manchester'.[160] He maintained the links between Manchester and London established by Rylands and strengthened by Spencer, being elected Master of the Company of Curriers in 1913. In him the capacity of the firm for winning the devotion of its staff received its most notable demonstration: when he retired at the age of ninety-five in 1916 he had completed seventy-six years of uninterrupted service with Rylands & Sons. When he died he had served for forty-five and a half years as a director. Service of such length ranked him with Theodore Taylor (1850–1952) of Batley in the annals of British business.[161]

During the Carnelley era (1901–15) average returns on capital fell only slightly to 4.33 per cent (Fig. 18). Dividends also sank slightly to 11.25 per cent and were maintained only by tapping reserves in fourteen out of the thirty-two half-years. Those reserves which had been increased by a half from £500,000 to £745,000 (1895–1903) were reduced in 1905 and again in 1908 to £700,000. During the whole of the Spencer-Carnelley era dividends more than doubled from 5.3 per cent (1873–88) to 11.8 per cent (1889–1915). Over the whole forty years from 1875 to 1914 they averaged 8.65 per cent, or nearly thrice the average return on consols. Such dividends exceeded the 8 per cent paid by the Royal

[159] JRL., Archives of Rylands & Sons Ltd, General Meetings Minute Book, 140, 11 Aug. 1890; 170, 8 Aug. 1892. *Northern Finance and Trade*, 22 Sept. 1897, 225.

[160] JRL., Archives of Rylands & Sons Ltd, General Meetings Minute Book, 345, 11 Aug. 1905, J.D. Wainwright.

[161] *Manchester Guardian*, 9 Oct. 1919, 3iv–v; *The Times*, 9 Oct. 1919, 13iii; 10 Oct., 7i; *Manchester City News*, 11 Oct. 1919, 9v.

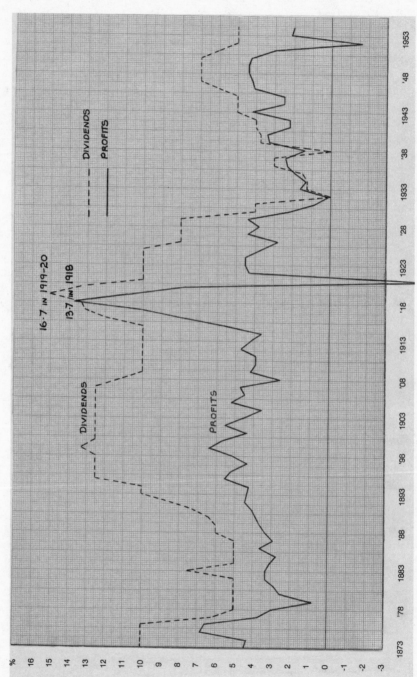

Figure 19: Profits and Dividends of Rylands & Sons Ltd, 1873–1954, based upon Table 2.
(John Rylands University Library of Manchester, Miss Judith Kent)

Table 2: Profits and dividends of Rylands & Sons Ltd, 1873–1954

Half year	Profits (£)	Capital (£)	Annual profit-ratio (%)	Annual rate of dividend (%)
1873	1,024,788	1,861,719		10
	46,150	2,114,267.88	4.4	10
1874	51,930.22	2,466,332.88		10
	66,320.81	2,755,363.7	4.3	10
1875	70,838.84	1,971,345.9		10
	66,435	2,006,651.4	6.8	10
1876	71,707.94	2,030,751.67		10
	74,866.7	2,219,563	6.6	10
1877	51,600.2	2,100,850.82		7.5
	28,865.98	2,166,015.93	3.7	5
1878	27,834.91	2,086,232.13		5
	37,546.13	2,142,979.51	3	5
1879	10,214.25	3,201,429.43		5
	15,130.14	3,103,375.4	0.8	5
1880	59,470.49	3,204,783		5
	18,892.29	3,132,202.66	2.5	5
1881	24,703.54	3,187,325		5
	61,234.52	3,114,053.21	2.8	5
1882	57,436.4	3,193,110.63		5
	49,253	3,223,497	3.3	5
1883	49,253	3,253,884.3		10
	57,199.96	3,242,685.42	3.3	5
1884	55,269.22	3,343,640.1		5
	47,451.47	3,338,049.48	3.1	5
1885	49,379.4	3,443,943.1		5
	42,490.1	3,416,185.6	2.7	5
1886	57,070.8	3,500,355.23		5
	67,525.84	3,464,909.43	3.6	5
1887	50,157.95	3,568,793.67		5
	51,929.63	3,518,265.83	2.9	5
1888	57,373.68	3,612,494.33		6
	59,845.46	3,591,759.65	3.3	6
1889	69,537.75	3,662,314.66		6
	69,496.2	3,829,003.23	3.6	6
1890	74,855.28	3,931,713		6.25
	74,102.13	3,904,318.1	3.8	6.5
1891	76,145.62	3,964,119.62		7
	82,206.6	3,919,000.42	4	7.5
1892	82,259.2	4,032,621.24		8
	88,652.62	3,846,783.43	4.4	9
1893	86,714.2	3,912,626		10
	80,946	3,893,792.36	4.3	10
1894	88,840.85	3,966,385.51		10
	84,276.48	4,109,226.2	4.2	10
1895	112,924.88	4,244,421.47		12.5
	117,866	4,220,150.58	5.5	12.5
1896	110,077.43	4,288,848.73		12.5
	110,887.99	4,275,246.25	5.2	12.5

Half year	Profits (£)	Capital (£)	Annual profit-ratio (%)	Annual rate of dividend (%)
1897	103,344.1	4,372,069.64		12.5
	82,875.43	4,316,891.67	4.3	12.5
1898	119,834.48	4,303,158.43		12.5
	98,953.26	4,280,512.81	5.1	12.5
1899	134,999.72	4,119,529.21		13.5
	128,771.96	4,111,794.2	6.4	13
1900	134,253.1	4,210,032.4		12.5
	103,298.38	4,196,994	5.7	12.5
1901	87,829.2	4,221,884.72		12.5
	92,097.5	4,179,623.48	4.3	12.5
1902	128,961.67	4,179,053.1		12.5
	106,587	4,257,427.55	5.5	12.5
1903	107,155.61	4,207,685.84		12.5
	81,637.95	4,212,187.53	4.5	12.5
1904	88,260.27	4,187,661.47		12.5
	58,187	4,085,977.41	3.6	12.5
1905	104,079.4	4,108,563.89		12.5
	113,951.77	4,159,945.14	5.2	12.5
1906	109,918.16	4,246,203.75		12.5
	82,121.68	4,223,544.6	4.5	12.5
1907	118,737.78	4,287,206.5		12.5
	79,258.48	4,233,507.75	4.7	12.5
1908	60,642.22	4,131,510.41		12.5
	41,019.25	3,922,574.55	2.6	10
1909	79,421.99	3,954,063.66		10
	85,168.45	3,912,084	4.2	10
1910	79,304.38	3,939,304.64		10
	68,639.98	3,841,625.85	3.9	10
1911	85,374.79	3,945,539.3		10
	66,670.7	3,896,985.38	3.9	10
1912	99,128.95	3,962,392.53		10
	87,709.62	3,937,073.61	4.7	10
1913	97,626.32	4,059,911.28		10
	66,305.23	3,936,345.13	4.2	10
1914	81,949.46	3,963,142.32		10
	55,179.55	3,826,870.98	3.6	10
1915	99,975.34	3,974,135.67		10
	120,032.92	3,949,570.86	5.6	10
1916	196,357.76	4,356,993.46		11.3
	146,128.5	4,343,253.11	7.9	12.7
1917	200,263.68	4,655,710.21		14.6
	290,142.94	4,882,018.22	10	11.6
1918	499,232.91	5,729,297.28		13.3
	247,087.44	5,456,143.84	13.7	13.3
1919	222,987.33	6,125,093.44		13.3
	506,699.52	6,751,254.43	10.8	16.7
1920	660,925.36	7,840,837.75		16.7
	−109,577.34	7,153,556.87	7.7	10
1921	−1,263,314.98	6,550,675.2		10
	65,038.1	5,633,464.35	−21.3	10
1922	111,954.8	5,563,038.22		10
	127,064.3	5,574,446.3	4.3	10

Half year	Profits (£)	Capital (£)	Annual profit-ratio (%)	Annual rate of dividend (%)
1923	129,590.59	5,586,117.85		10
	125,664.41	5,645,295.63	4.5	10
1924	141,600.12	5,647,893.1		10
	114,443.67	5,637,159.93	4.5	10
1925	97,776.94	5,585,971.58		10
	106,553.46	5,529,752.67	3.7	10
1926	85,654.97	5,430,086.33		8
	66,107.8	5,344,157.12	2.8	8
1927	103,813.79	5,322,967.28		8
	133,816.11	5,344,029.1	4.4	8
1928	199,350.55	5,275,296.64	3.8	8
1929	225,907.86	5,112,380.44	4.4	8
1930	106,892.59	4,860,139.73	2.2	4
1931	45,079.95	5,068,053.19	0.9	4
1932	3,927.13	3,968,460.1	0.1	Nil
1933	63,551.62	3,892,579.5	1.6	1.25
1934	49,366.15	3,841,029.79	1.3	1.25

Year ending
19 Jan.

Half year	Profits (£)	Capital (£)	Annual profit-ratio (%)	Annual rate of dividend (%)
1936	70,975	3,774,595.69	1.9	1.5
1937	90,796.48	3,891,034.1	2.3	3
1938	93,092.28	3,904,598.1	2.4	3
1939	53,625.87	3,755,125.27	1.4	Nil
1940	130,485.77	4,009,634.1	3.3	3.75
1941	147,900.26	4,354,608.73	3.4	3.75
1942	102,404.85	4,645,853.67	2.2	4
1943	95,568.85	4,345,391.52	2.2	4
1944	180,160.39	4,321,561.43	4.2	5
1945	111,960	4,539,649	2.5	5
1946	121,057	4,792,447	2.5	5
1947	202,345	4,960,563	4.1	6
1948	214,684	5,151,761	4.2	7
1949	224,333	5,074,351	4.4	7
1950	239,993	5,430,603	4.4	7
1951	243,836	5,615,597	4.3	7
1952	166,906	5,607,524	3.0	6
1953	−81,240	5,147,724	−1.6	5
1954	118,665	5,597,830	2.1	5
1955	169,493	8,494,662	1.7	5

Source: John Rylands Library, Archives of Rylands & Sons Ltd, Auditors' Balance Book, 1873–1950. The balance sheets were printed from 1904 and modified in format from 1944. The last financial year covers fourteen months, ending on 31 March 1955. The preceding graph (Fig. 19) clearly reveals the contrast between the relatively stable dividends and the fluctuating returns on capital.

Exchange and by the Fine Cotton Spinners' and Doublers' Association, which was until 1930 the most successful combine within the cotton industry. That standard of prosperity was maintained until the black year of 1921.

11. The decline and demise of Rylands & Sons Ltd, 1921–89

The turnover of businesses in the textile trade remained very high. What proved remarkable was not the ultimate dissolution of the firm but its survival for over a hundred and thirty years. When Carnelley retired in 1916 the eight remaining directors mustered an average period of service of some forty-six years. No fundamental change in either business strategy or tactics took place under the administration of Carnelley's five successors.

The cotton industry reached its apogee during the great boom of 1920. The firm of Rylands & Sons however reached its own climacteric during the years 1917–19 under the chairmanship of William F. Bewley (1845–1929) when it generated average profits of 11.5 per cent in contrast to a rate of 7.7 per cent in 1920 (Fig. 18). That achievement was the result not of active enterprise but of the wartime inflation of prices which compelled the firm increasingly to finance its own clients and to enhance the value of its stocks. By 1920 its balance sheet revealed two dangerous imbalances: 53 per cent of its assets were in the form of debts and another 33 per cent were in the form of stocks.

During the boom of 1920 the firm transformed its financial structure for the first time since 1873: in July 1920 it doubled its capital to £4,000,000, one half of which was issued in £1 shares and one half in 8 per cent cumulative preference shares. In the subsequent collapse of the postwar boom it lost £1,263,000 during the first half of 1921 as its stocks depreciated in value, necessitating a massive reduction in reserves by one-third. The directors finally closed down Gorton Mills in 1921, after it had suffered losses for seventeen years, and opened branches in Newcastle in 1923 and in Birmingham in 1929 in order to extend the home trade. Its prospects continued to be adversely affected by the decline of the drapery trade, aggravated by the mass-production of ready-made clothing for women and by its skilful marketing through the new department stores. In 1926 the firm reduced its dividend below the level of 10 per cent for the first time since 1892 and it began to introduce a number of economies. From 1928 it ended the rare and commendable practice of publishing complete half-yearly accounts.[162] The Longford Buildings on Oxford Street were sold in 1929 and the Gidlow Works were converted to electric drive. Returns on capital were halved during the 1920s. Dividends were

---

[162] *Statist*, 7 Feb. 1925, 230.

nevertheless maintained. Average dividends during the next decade (1930–39) sank however to 1.4 per cent per annum and equalled for the first time the average return on capital. The doubling of the firm's capital in 1920 reduced the average return in 1920–29 to one-fifth of the industry's average rate and in 1930–38 to one-quarter of that rate of return.[163] Nil dividends were declared in 1932 and in 1939. By 1929 the whole balance of financial power between Manchester and London had shifted decisively and irrevocably in favour of London. In that year Rylands & Sons were compelled for the first time in their history to appoint a chairman from outside the ranks of the firm. Bewley's two successors had both been recruited from the ranks: William Gregson had fifty-three years of service and William Branson fifty-two such years. William Gregson (1855–1927) rose from the position of office boy in 1866 through that of company secretary to that of chairman (1919–25).[164] In 1921 he boldly but vainly proposed the appointment of a chemist to the board of directors: his nominee W.N. Haworth (1883–1950) won the Nobel Prize in 1937. In the hope of bringing financial salvation to the firm the accountant J.J.D. Hourston was recruited from Glasgow and served as chairman from 1929 to 1933 but failed to rejuvenate the firm and was forced out of office. The most notable event of his term of office was the construction (1929–32) of a new nine-storeyed warehouse, which had its foundation stone laid on 28 February 1930. That building was designed by H.S. Fairhurst (1868–1945) and was the most imposing commercial structure to be built in Manchester since the warehouse of S. & J. Watts in 1856–58: it was surmounted by an aircraft beacon, which was visible for some sixty miles.[165] Hourston was succeeded by Edward Rhodes (1870–1959) who was a partner in the firm of Sir Jacob Behrens & Sons and an export merchant.[166] Rhodes served as chairman from 1933 until 1953, or for a longer period than any of his predecessors. He failed, however, to reform the 'complex of inefficiency and muddle' which he had inherited.[167] He preferred to pursue his own personal ambitions, serving in 1937 as the President of the Manchester Chamber of Commerce.

Trading conditions improved temporarily with the outbreak of war in 1939 and with the postwar boom. The average return on capital however between 1940 and 1954 at 2.9 per cent was just

163 P.E. Hart, *Studies in profit, business saving and investment in the U.K., 1920–62* (Allen & Unwin, 1965), i, 121.

164 *Textile Mercury*, 74, 17 April 1926, 360; *Manchester City News*, 15 January 1927, 12vi.

165 *Manchester Guardian*, 29 September 1931, 7, 'An air beacon for Manchester'.

166 *Textile Weekly*, 19 May 1933, 281.

167 M. Dupree (ed.) *Lancashire and Whitehall: the diary of Sir Raymond Streat* (Manchester: University Press, 1987), i (1931–39), 239, 12 May 1933.

over one-third of what it had been during the golden age of 1889–1915 while the average dividend of 5.4 per cent per annum was only one quarter. The end of the postwar boom brought nemesis in its wake to the whole of the British cotton industry. Rylands & Sons proved to be no exception. During 1952 the firm's export trade to Australasia collapsed. In 1953 it suffered its first absolute losses since the black year of 1921, paying no dividend. On 19 November 1953 Great Universal Stores Ltd (G.U.S.), which had been established in Manchester in 1900, announced their successful purchase of 97 per cent of the firm's ordinary shares. The take-over of 1953 was the ultimate price paid for incorporation in 1873. Isaac Wolfson (1897–1991) became chairman from 19 November 1953 and decided to concentrate upon the wholesale business of the firm, selling off the Heapey Works and the freehold of the great Manchester warehouse. In 1967 the firm moved out of High Street to the Gorse Mill at Chadderton,[168] which had been bought in 1966. In 1971 G.U.S. ceased active trading under the name of Rylands & Sons Ltd but retained the name, with an office at 3 Dale Street, the headquarters of G.U.S. Merchandise Corporation Ltd. On 8 May 1989 the name of the firm was finally removed from the Register of Companies, so ending the saga which had begun in St Helens in 1819.

12. Surviving memorials to John Rylands and to Enriqueta Augustina Rylands

The communication
Of the dead is tongued with fire beyond the language of the living
T.S. Eliot, 'Little Gidding' (1942)

In 1658 Sir Thomas Browne warned his readers that, 'to extend our memories by monuments' contradicted the basic tenets of the Christian faith. The same message was reiterated by Shelley, by Tennyson, by Arnold and by Kipling. Its burden remains plain and unambiguous: any aspiration to perpetuate a particular name is doomed to suffer shipwreck at the all-destroying hands of Time. What remains remarkable in the case of John Rylands is not that so many of the memorials to him have perished but that some at least have so far survived the siege of envious Time, especially in the three boroughs of Wigan, Trafford and Manchester. Today his name is more widely known than it ever was during his own lifetime. The reason is not to be found in any official policy of the local corporation: the city of Manchester has no public statue of John Rylands, no civic plaque upon any building and as yet no 'Rylands trail' for the visual education of its schoolchildren. The

---

[168] *Manchester Evening News*, 24 Oct. 1967, 11 'Textile firm are quitting the city'.

reason is rather to be found in the establishment of a great private library and in the worldwide expansion of the English language which has carried the influence of that library around the globe. It is an appropriate time to take stock of those monuments to a remarkable person which have not yet been destroyed, as have most of the firm's mills. Of the great complex of mills at Gorton only the Wadding Works of 1894 remains standing on the site occupied in 1993 by Lynton Commercial Units Ltd (Hadleigh Industries Group). The tower block of Abbey Court has been built upon part of the site but nearby streets still bear the name of Rylands, Longford and Gidlow. Wigan still retains a magnificent and memorable building in the Gidlow Works. Those mills were taken over first by G.U.S. and then by the local corporation. They never became a listed building but from 1984 were incorporated into a conservation area. From 1989 they were occupied by the Wigan College of Technology, to the Building Fund of which in 1902 Rylands & Sons had contributed £250. The mills were then inexplicably renamed the Pagefield Building.

In London the Rylands Hall inaugurated in Tottenham Court Road in 1908 was destroyed by enemy action in 1944. In the Isle of Wight three institutions survive but in a different guise: Longford House at Haven Street has become a mental hospital for women, the Longford Institute has become a nursing home and Corston House in Ryde has been converted into a complex of flats. In Stretford Longford Hall lost its function and became the object of bitter public controversy. During the years 1911 to 1982 it remained under the management of the local authority. It suffered severely from the ravages of time and required from 1984 the support of external scaffolding. In 1988 a local charitable trust dedicated to ensuring its preservation was founded and secured its official listing as a grade II building. The new Trafford Borough Council, which had absorbed the functions of that of Stretford from 1974, decided in 1984 to demolish the hall. That decision was reaffirmed in 1992 in defiance of local opinion. The terrace of six cottages built in 1877 at Sunnyside in the grounds of the park survives in as sturdy a condition as the eight Longford Cottages built to the rear of the hall. The nearby Longford Institute has however been demolished,[169] like the public baths and the coffee house built by John Rylands. The Town Hall which he built in 1878 has escaped the threat of demolition and survives as the Stretford Civic Theatre. Stretford Congregational Chapel, whose foundation stone he laid in 1861, was demolished in 1961. The Union Chapel built on Edge Lane near Longford Hall in 1867, with a memorial

---

[169] On Kenwood Road part of the boundary wall and an iron pillar by the entrance to its former grounds remained standing in 1993.

plate commemorating its restoration in 1890 by Mrs Rylands, began however to undergo reconstruction from 1989 as a commercial office complex renamed 'Rylands Hall.'

Outside Stretford other memorials remain in Cheadle Hulme and in the city itself. Cheadle Hulme School was endowed in 1873 with funds for the John Rylands Jubilee prizes for its scholars: in 1909 its board room acquired a memorial medallion sculpted by John Adams Acton (1834–1910). In Hulme the Stretford Road Congregational Church had its foundation stone laid by the twin brother of Mrs Rylands, on the site of the Zion Chapel inaugurated in 1858. As the Zion Institute it still stands upon Zion Crescent, with an inscription on a bronze tablet in the foyer which reads:

> This Church
> erected on the site
> of the old Zion
> Chapel through the
> munificence of the late
> Mrs E.A. Rylands of
> Longford Hall, Stretford,
> was opened on
> October 11th 1911

At number 244 Deansgate the Congregational Church House inaugurated in 1911 was sold in 1985 by the Lancashire Congregational Union: it was then renamed Deansgate Court and converted into an office complex. On the second floor of the building the former Milton Hall is now used by the Church of Jesus Christ of Latter Day Saints but still preserves on its right-hand wall a teak plaque unveiled in 1911 by the Revd J.W. Kiddle, secretary to Mrs Rylands, and inscribed as follows:

> This Church House
> which is intended to serve as a centre
> of Congregational activity and
> influence is a memorial to the wise and
> large-hearted munificence of the late
> Mrs Enriqueta Augustina Rylands
> of Longford Hall in this County. Who, by
> the Gift of the Site and a Donation of
> Half the Sum Required for the Building
> Made its Erection Possible.

The Rylands Vault at Upholland, containing the remains of J.G. Rylands and of his wife, Hannah, and perhaps also those of his uncle Richard Rylands and of his wife Elizabeth, had deteriorated by 1904 into a neglected state,[170] disappearing thereafter. John

---

[170] JRL., Archives of Rylands & Sons Ltd, Minutes of the Board of Directors, iv, 220, 1 July 1904.

Rylands himself had always attributed his own achievements to the influence of his mother. The family's memorial to Elizabeth Rylands in Gidlow Lane School survived from 1830 until 1898 when it was demolished. The memorial tablet to Mrs Rylands was however preserved in the nearby Congregational Chapel (Fig. 2). What happened to the Rylands Vault beneath the floor of the school, containing in unconsecrated ground the unbaptized remains of the four infants of John and Dinah Rylands, remains as yet unknown. The grave of the first two wives of John Rylands, Dinah and Martha, was destroyed in 1955 when Rusholme Road Cemetery in Manchester was converted into an open space (Fig. 20). The third and greatest of the Rylands Vaults remains intact and undisturbed, eloquent in its serenity (Figs 21–23). Its condition provides a sharp contrast to the neglected grave of Charles Hallé in Weaste Cemetery. The centenary of the death of John Rylands in 1988 was commemorated in different ways by the University of Manchester, by British Rail and by the Stretford Local History Society. The University created the John Rylands Research Institute and the Library published a special centenary issue of its *Bulletin*. British Rail placed in service a Mark 3 Pullman locomotive named 'John Rylands' on the Piccadilly – Euston service. Finally at Stretford Public Library a special exhibition was organized, devoted to the life and labours of John Rylands. The main institution in Manchester still preserving the name of John Rylands has become the University. The Department of Theology has retained the chair of Biblical Exegesis created in 1904, renamed the Rylands Chair in 1908 and occupied by four of the century's most eminent theologians.[171] The University Library merged in 1972 with the John Rylands Library. Thereafter two memorials were transferred from Deansgate to the University Library, the full-length painting of John Rylands presented in 1869 to Martha Rylands and Cassidy's maquette of 1907 for the statue of Mrs Rylands, which being placed in the Muriel Stott Centre of the Library has sometimes been mistaken for a statue of Muriel Stott. As for the library founded by Mrs Rylands it has triumphantly survived the challenges presented in nine successive decades. The function fulfilled by libraries is one of recent origin, since most of Europe's great libraries date back only to the Renaissance of the fifteenth century: Verona remains unique as the seat of the oldest library in the world, the Capitular Library established in the fifth century A.D.[172] The John Rylands Library may be relatively new but it has resisted the erosion of

---

[171] A.S. Peake (1904–29), C.H. Dodd (1930–35), T.W. Manson (1936–58) and F.F. Bruce (1959–78), who were followed by Barnabas Lindars (1978–90).
[172] A.R.A. Hobson, *Great libraries* (Weidenfeld, 1970).

function suffered by other foundations.[173] Indeed its expansion has proved to be truly remarkable. The two great foundation-collections of 1892 and 1901 have been reinforced by a series of purchases, deposits and gifts, including from the 1920s the muniments of many of the leading families of the region. It may not have become a copyright library but it has benefited extensively from successive generous donations. Its history remains one of the great success stories in the cultural history of the century. As a repository of material covering a broad spectrum of all the liberal arts and a virtual microcosm of the humanities, it has become one of the great libraries of the world and especially a library for the international community of scholars. Since 1972 its name has been extended to the main University Library on Burlington Street. On Deansgate in the heart of the city the original building remains even more impressive today than it was in 1899, attracting visitors in increasing numbers. The man commemorated by that library had achieved much during his own lifetime in improving the material conditions of people, in elevating their ideals and in championing the defenceless. 'He was always ready to stand up and fight for the weak.'[174] His name has been preserved to posterity, as Enriqueta Rylands intended that it should be. Her primary purpose, set forth in a manner which John Rylands himself would have appreciated, was expressed in one of the twenty-eight mottoes decorating the nave of the library: *Perpetui fructum donavi nominis* – 'I have bestowed the gift of an enduring name'. In commemorating her husband Mrs Rylands also created her own memorial, inspiring a prophecy which has proved fully justified. 'Mr and Mrs John Rylands will be loved and honoured so long as Manchester endures.'[175]

[173] *New Society*, 28 March 1974, 778–80, E.P. Thompson, 'In citizens' bad books'. W.J. West, *The strange rise of semi-literate England: the dissolution of the libraries* (Duckworth, 1991).
[174] [S.G. Green], *In memoriam John Rylands* (1889), 8.
[175] *Methodist Recorder*, XLIX:2622, 20 Feb. 1908, 3, 'Mrs Rylands's bequests'.

Figure 20: Gravestone of Dinah Rylands (1801–43) and Martha Rylands (1806–75).
The stone was destroyed in 1955 when Rusholme Road Cemetery was converted into an open space. The grave contained not only the mortal remains of the first two wives of John Rylands but also those of the infant Emily and of his son and heir, William Rylands (1828–61). The text is taken from 1 Thess. 4:14: 'them also which sleep in Jesus will God bring with him'.

(JRL, Library Archives)

THE RYLANDS TOMB.

Figure 21: Rylands Memorial in Southern Cemetery, Manchester, in 1892
In the vast expanse of Southern Cemetery one grave stands out above all others. For thirty-five years it was surmounted by an elaborate structure resembling the Albert Memorial. The plan of the memorial was completed on 16 May 1889 by the architect C.H. Heathcote (1850–1938) of the firm of Heathcote & Rawle. The structure was completed in 1892 and was surmounted at each corner by an angel with a golden trumpet. The gold attracted vandals in 1927, whereafter the structure was dismantled. In 1967 vandals struck again, stealing the enclosing bronze railings (*Manchester Evening News*, 17 Dec. 1969, 7, 'Raiders plunder famous grave'). In 1993 the architect's plans were deposited for safe custody in the John Rylands Library.
(*JRL, Library Archives, Newspaper Cuttings, ii, 128, from Manchester Dispatch, 8 Feb. 1908*)

Figure 22: Tomb of John Rylands.

The grave of John Rylands lies in the unconsecrated portion of the cemetery in a plot of land 27 feet square and occupying 18 vault spaces, which were purchased in succession on 2 January, 6 March and 1 May 1889. It is surmounted by a marble and granite monument, inscribed with the following texts:

- i. Redeemed with the precious blood of Christ. (1 *Pet.*, 1:18–19)
- ii. Not slothful in business; fervent in spirit; serving the Lord. (*Rom.*, 12:11)
- iii. The Lord stood with me and strengthened me. (2 *Tim.*, 4:17).
- iv. Kept by the power of God, through faith unto salvation. (1 *Pet.*, 1:5)
- v. Looking for the mercy of our Lord Jesus Christ unto eternal life. (*Jude*, 21)
- vi. They shall be mine, saith the Lord of Hosts, in that day when I make up my jewels (*Mal.*, 3:17).

The vault beneath is walled in white enamelled brick and contains the single coffin with its companion urn, the remains of Mrs Rylands having been cremated. The grave is flanked by that of Fanny Huckett and is faced by that of William Carnelley, who was buried, beneath a stone surmounted by a spire, close to his friend and employer.

(J.G. Farnie Esq., 1992)

Figure 23: Memorial Inscription to John Rylands.

The inscription complements that to Enriqueta Rylands on the other side of the sarcophagus. Both bear the same legend: 'In Loving Memory'.

(J.G. Farnie Esq., 1992)

13. Publications by John Rylands, 1861–87

1. 'An address delivered by John Rylands Esq. on the occasion of his laying the foundation stone of the Congregational Church Stretford, on March 29th 1861', in Joseph Parker (ed.) *Our Own,* i (1861), 112–13.

2. *The Holy Bible containing the Old and New Testaments, arranged in paragraphs* (Manchester: Cave & Sever, 1863, 1272 pp.)

   The New Testament was apparently printed first, the title page being dated 1862. The 5,810 paragraphs of the whole Bible were divided between the 4,404 paragraphs in the Old Testament and the 1,406 paragraphs in the New Testament. Similarly the 1,272 pages were divided into two sections of 968 and 304 pages.

   The two later editions of 1878 and 1886 were shorter, with only 1,240 pages. They based their text upon that edited by Dr F.H. Scrivener in the Cambridge Paragraph Bible of 1873. They were printed by Unwin Bros at Chilworth. The 1886 edition was arranged in two columns because many readers had found the length of the lines in the two earlier editions inconvenient.

3. *An index designed to accompany the Holy Bible in paragraphs, to help the enquirer to ascertain what saith the Scriptures* (London: R. Clay & Sons, n.d. 51 + 226pp.)

   The index comprised four separate parts, an index to the Books of the Old Testament in thirty-eight pages, one to the Books of the New Testament in thirteen pages, an index to the subjects of the Bible extending to 215 pages and, finally, an alphabetical list of subjects in ten pages, each containing five columns. The index was reprinted in 1886 by Unwin Bros at Chilworth and was shortened to 192 pages.

4. *The Cavendish hymnal, compiled for use in homes and churches.* (Bucklersbury, London: George Unwin, 1864)

   The two-page preface by Joseph Parker, dated 12 November, 1863, acknowledged 'the noble liberality' of John Rylands as the main inspiring force behind the hymnal. He had supplied nearly 30,000 hymns for the consideration of the committee: he had also paid the full cost incurred by 'the enormous manual labour of preparing the selection for the press'. That selection amounted to fourfold the number included in the first edition of *Hymns ancient and modern* (1861). It comprised 900 hymns, seventy-four chants (including fifty psalms) and thirty-eight anthems. The analytical arrangement of the hymns in twenty distinct sections, with twenty-eight sub-headings, may very probably be attributed to John Rylands. At the end of the volume were fifteen pages of indexes, an eight-page index of first lines, a six-page index of texts of Scripture, and, because the hymnal contained only words without music, a single page index of peculiar metres. J. Julian mentioned five hundred books of English hymns in his *Dictionary of hymnology* (Murray, 1892, 1907), 260 and dismissed the *Cavendish hymnal* as 'a heavy production on the old lines and a failure'.

5. *Il Nuovo Testamento del Nostro Signore e Salvatore Gesu Criste tradotto in lingua italiana da Giovanni Diodati* (Londra: La Societa Biblica Britannica e Forestiere, 1867, 238pp.).

   This translation, made in 1603, was printed and distributed after the foundation in 1866 of the La Spezia Mission for Italy. It was reprinted in 1872 as the first publication of the Italian Bible Society which had been established at Rome in 1871.

6. *Le Nouveau Testament de Notre Seigneur Jésus-Christ: version de J.F.Ostervald. Nouvelle édition revue* (Londres: La Société Biblique Britannique et Étrangère, 1869, 524pp.).

   This edition of the text of 1724 was a reprint of the 1855 edition and was itself reprinted in 1870 with 504 pages.

7. *Hymns of the Church Universal. In two parts. I. – The spirit of the psalms. II. – General hymns, with prefaces, annotations and indexes* (Chilworth: Unwin Bros, 1885, printed for private circulation).

   The preface, the introductions to the successive sections, the notes and the biographical index were written by Dr S.G. Green (*Baptist Handbook*, 1906, 441). Dr Green very probably wrote the preface to the thirty-four volumes of hymns collected down to the year 1900 and presented in 1905, with a nine-volume index, to the John Rylands Library.

8. *Hymns for the young, presented for the use of young people meeting in the town hall, Stretford* (Chilworth: Unwin Bros, 1887).

   This work was intended for use in Sunday Schools, especially on the anniversary occasions which became frequent in Lancashire during the 1880s.

9. A French hymnal, prepared for the use of the Belleville Mission in Paris of Miss de Broën (*In memoriam John Rylands*, 1889, 37–8).

14. Chronology of the life of John Rylands

1761
16 Oct   Birth of Elizabeth Pilkington (1761–1829) at Horwich Moor.

1767
19 Feb.   Birth of Joseph Rylands (1767–1847) at Parr.

1793

Marriage of Elizabeth Pilkington and Joseph Rylands.

1801
7 Feb.   Birth of John Rylands at Parr.

1812
11 March   Lease to Joseph Rylands, check manufacturer, of the premises called Glovers in Hardshaw, St Helens, for use as a draper's shop. The lease was renewed until 1824.

1819

Foundation of the partnership of Rylands & Sons by Joseph Rylands, at the age of 52, with his three sons, Joseph, Richard and John.

1821
19 July   The new partnership established a handloom weaving shop in St Helens behind Church St (*St Helens Reporter*, 21 Oct. 1921, a reference I owe to Mrs Diana K. Jones).

1822
24 May   Purchase of a plot of land fronting High Street in Manchester.

1823
22 Dec.   John Rylands began business in Manchester, at No. 11, New High Street, a street which disappeared from the map during the 1860s as the firm progressively engrossed neighbouring properties and even whole thoroughfares.

1824
24 June   John Rylands became a subscriber to the Portico Library in Manchester and remained such for 21 months until 6 April 1826.

1825

17 March   Marriage of John Rylands to Dinah Raby, only daughter of William and Dinah Raby, at St John's Church, Manchester.

19 Oct.   Conveyance of Buckley House Estate and Gidlow Estate of 110 acres at Wigan to Joseph Rylands, Richard Pilkington and Thomas Pilkington, followed by the construction of the Wigan Linen Works.

1826

20 May   Birth of John Garthwaite Rylands, eldest son.

1827

22 Feb.   Mortgage of the two estates at Wigan for £10,000 to William Raby, father-in-law of John Rylands.

1827–34

John Rylands resided in Wigan after a period of residence (1825–27) in Manchester.

1828

1 Jan.   Birth of William Rylands, second son.

1829

9 May   Death of Elizabeth Rylands, mother of John Rylands, at the age of 68.

1830

10 Jan.   Death of Joseph Rylands, third son aged 6 months, and his burial at Gidlow Lane School in Wigan.

1831

John Rylands became a member of the Manchester Exchange, retaining his membership until 1877 (Manchester Central Library, Archives Department, M 81/7/2, a reference I owe to Miss Jean M. Ayton, the City Archivist).

22 March   Purchase by firm of 88 bags of 'bowed' cotton and the sale on 27 May of cotton twist.

4 July   Birth of twin daughters, Eliza and Emily.

1832

10 Jan.   Death of Eliza Rylands.

3 Feb.   Death of Emily Rylands and the burial of the twins at Gidlow Lane School.

12 July   Death of Eliza Rylands II, stillborn.

1834
4 Dec.   Death of Emily Rylands II, fourth daughter and last child of John Rylands at the age of 6 months, and her burial at Rusholme Road Cemetery in Manchester.

1839
21 Jan.   Lease of the King Coal and Cannel Mines at Wigan. Purchase of a cotton mill at Ainsworth.

1840

              John Rylands was first listed as a member of the Manchester Chamber of Commerce.
16 Nov.   He became a shareholder in the Portico Library.

1842
1 Oct.   Joseph Rylands Senior of Wigan and John Rylands of Manchester dissolved their partnership (*London Gazette*, 28 Nov. 1843, 4095ii.).

24 Nov.   Lease of Gorton Mills at an annual rent of £2,150 from John Chapman of Mottram (Chapman Deeds in the Manchester Central Library listed at M95, Box 8).

1 Dec.   Purchase of all the machinery in Gorton Mills from John Chapman for £7,789 18*s*. 2*d*., a purchase witnessed by George Hadfield.

1843
31 May   Birth of Enriqueta Augustina Tennant at Havana. Her father died in 1848 and her mother in 1855. Her stepfather committed suicide in 1869.

15 Aug.   Death of Dinah Rylands at the age of 40, leaving two sons, and her burial in Rusholme Road Cemetery.

1844
June   Gorton Mills began working under John Rylands (J. Higson, *The Gorton Historical Recorder*, 1852, 192).

1845

              John Rylands declined to join in the schism within the Manchester Chamber of Commerce, which created a rival institution in the Manchester Commercial Association. He also refused to become a county magistrate.

11 May   Subscription of £100 to building fund of Cavendish Street Congregational Church, followed by three more donations in 1846–50 totalling £220. (Manchester Central Library Archives Department, M162, Cavendish Street Church Manchester Subscription Accounts, 1845–53).

1846

After the death of Dinah Rylands, John Rylands leased a large house at Hoylake by the mouth of the Dee, bought a handsome 30-ton yacht and there entertained his senior employees as well as Dr Robert Halley (1796–1876), his minister at both Mosley St and Cavendish St.

30 Nov.   Report on the Employees of Gorton Mills by John Rylands to Leonard Horner. (Printed in full in *In memoriam John Rylands* (1889), 20, and summarized in the *Factory Inspectors' Reports*, 31 Oct. 1846, 7).

1847

Establishment of a fustian department, under William Carnelley.

6 Jan.   General Provision Stores opened at Gorton Mill (Higson, 196).

10 Feb.   Reuben Spencer entered the employment of the firm.

21 May   J.G. Rylands attained his majority, an occasion celebrated at Gorton Villa and Mill (Higson, 197).

6 July   Death of Joseph Rylands Senior, father of John Rylands and alderman of Wigan, at Gidlow House at the age of 80.

1848

4 Jan.   Marriage of John Rylands to Martha Carden, daughter of Isaac Greenough, brewer of Parr, at St Peter's Church, Newton.

22 Jan.   John Rylands presided as chairman at a soirée of the Fairfield & Droylsden Naturalists' Society and Mechanics' Institute (Higson, 200).

2 May   Indenture concluded between John Rylands and his eldest son, J.G. Rylands, assigning him the interest on the sum of £10,000.

1849

Opening of a warehouse in Cheapside, London, under Carnelley.

14 Aug.   Vote of thanks to John Rylands at the Church Inn, Droylsden, for his strict compliance with the Ten Hours' Act (Higson, 204).

31 Oct.   Strike by power loom weavers at Gorton, which lasted for two months until 2 Jan. 1850.

1850

30 June   The five executors of the late Joseph Rylands dissolved their partnership on the withdrawal of Joseph Rylands, the eldest son (*London Gazette*, 21 Jan. 1851, 156).

1851

4 Sept.   John and Martha Rylands were received into membership of Cavendish St Congregational Church.

22 Dec.   Agreement between John Rylands and his son William, identical to that of 1848.

1852

John Rylands was joined in business by his second son, William.

1853

Establishment of a fancy goods department.

27 May   Death of Joseph Rylands (1796–1853), eldest brother of John Rylands, at the age of 56.

23 Nov.   J.G. Rylands of Orrell, eldest son of John, signed his will, leaving his whole estate to his wife Hannah Bertenshaw.

1854

John Rylands withdrew from the Wigan Linen Works.

1 March   Fire at the Manchester warehouse caused a net loss of £40,000: the premises were rebuilt within a year.

13 March   Mortgage of part of Gorton Mills to John Chapman for £7,776.

1855

1 Nov.   Purchase of Longford Hall and its estate of 43 acres in Hedge Lane, Stretford, from C.J.S. Walker J.P., (1788–1875) the senior county magistrate for £8,900. The property was mortgaged on 5 Nov. 1855 for £6,000 to Herbert and Henry Birley.

1856

Transfer of London premises from Cheapside to Wood St.

27 Sept.   Dissolution of partnership of three remaining executors of Joseph Rylands at Wigan (*London Gazette*, 3 Oct. 1856, 3263).

1857

John Rylands transferred his residence from Ardwick Green to Longford Hall. He served as high constable of Salford Hundred.

1858

6 March   John Rylands assigned William Rylands £5,000.

11 May   John Cross of Wigan secured the King Coal, Cannel and Arley Mines.

24 Nov.   John Rylands moved a vote of congratulations at the annual meeting of the Manchester and Salford Asylum for Female Penitents upon its success, especially in its industrial operations.

1859

William Rylands became the business partner of his father.

1860
26 March   Agreement of partnership between Richard Rylands, John Rylands and John Cross to carry on business as Rylands & Cross at Wigan.
21 Nov.   John Rylands was elected a Fellow of the Society of Arts. In 1861 he became a guarantor for the International Exhibition of 1862.
11 Dec.   Inundation of the Red House Colliery of Thomas Fletcher of Ainsworth (1805–93) by water escaping from the newly-constructed mill lodge of John Rylands, Fletcher issuing a writ for damages on 4 Nov. 1861.

1861
29 March   John Rylands laid, on Good Friday, the foundation stone of Stretford Congregational Church.
21 Nov.   Death of William Rylands, the unmarried son and heir of John Rylands, at the age of 33 and his interment in his mother's grave at Rusholme Road Cemetery.

1862
3 Sept.   The case of *Rylands v. Fletcher* was heard at the Liverpool Summer Assizes.

1863
23 Feb.   Richard Rylands (1798–1863), sole surviving brother of John Rylands signed his will, appointing John Rylands and John Cross as executors.
11 March   Death of Richard Rylands at Orrell.
1 June   Appointment of John Rylands as a member of the sub-committee on the *Cavendish hymnal*, published in 1864.

1864
8 March   Lease of Water Street Mills.
24 June   Purchase of Medlock Mills for £3,300.
23 Aug.   Purchase of Gorton Mills from John Chapman (1810–77), M.P. for Grimsby, for £25,000.

1865

Purchase of Oxford Road Twist Co. (*Manchester Guardian*, 10 Jan. 1883, 5vi.).

25 March   Conveyance of two houses on Burlington St to William Woodward and John Rylands for £700. Woodward surrendered his interest on 11 May 1868 and John Rylands made three further purchases totalling 19 houses on the same street between 14 April 1866 and 23 June 1874 for £440.

5 April   Formation of the Union Church, Stretford, under the patronage of John Rylands.

10 May   Conveyance of the Egyptian Buildings Block on Market St & High St to Rylands & Spencer.

1866

Appointment of William Linnell (1837–1901) as his private secretary (*Manchester City News*, 1 March 1901).

7 March   Lease of an office in Liverpool from the Corporation for a peppercorn rent.

14 May   The Court of Exchequer Chamber in the case of *Rylands v. Fletcher* rendered a verdict for the plaintiff, Thomas Fletcher. Damages to be paid by John Rylands were agreed on 18 June.

14 June   Angel Hotel Block on Market St conveyed to Rylands & Spencer.

20 June   Angel Hotel Block mortgaged to the vendor, John Dugdale.

1867

2 Jan.   Inauguration of Union Chapel on Edge Lane, Stretford.

3 April   Deed of partnership between John Rylands and Reuben Spencer.

24 June   Purchase of Primrose Mill, Walkden Moor, for £10,000.

4 Oct.   Great meeting at Cavendish St Congregational Church addressed by John Rylands in the hope of persuading Dr Parker to decline an invitation from London and to remain in Manchester (*Manchester Guardian*, 29 Nov. 1902, 7iii).

2 Dec.   Trust Deed of Union Chapel, Stretford.

1868

28 Feb.   Destructive fire at Ainsworth Mills, the 'Coach and Horse Factory', causing £5,000 of damage and leading to their abandonment.

11 May   Purchase of Horwich Vale Print Works, mortgaged the next day to the vendor, John Chippendale.

June   John Rylands presented Dr Parker on his departure
                from Manchester with a Bible (*The British Monthly*,
                Feb. 1903, 117, 'Dr Parker's Bible').

17 July   The House of Lords delivered the final ruling in the
                case of *Rylands v. Fletcher* after three successive
                judgments rendered in the lower courts since 1862.
                The ruling established a new principle in the law of
                tort, making a defendant strictly liable for any damage
                caused in consequence of his actions, irrespective of
                whether he had or had not been negligent (*Law Journal
                Reports*, 37, n.s., 1868 Common Law, Court of
                Exchequer, Trinity Term 1868, 161–6, Lord Cairns
                and Lord Cranworth).

7 Nov.   Purchase of the site for a branch office in Liverpool for
                £30,000, on the corner of St George's Place and Roe
                Street, facing St George's Hall.

1869
12 April   Lease of Silvester's Block on Market St for £1,050 per
                annum.
13–29 May   Strike at the Gidlow Works by the self-actor minders
                (JRL., English Manuscript 1185, ii, 51).

1870
July   Strike at the Gorton Mills by the self-actor minders.
1 Oct.   Lease of the Heapey Bleach Works.

1871
2 March   Lease by John Rylands of 46 Argyll Rd, Kensington,
                from Spencer Herapath for £110 per annum.
28 June   John Rylands attended the opening of the Manchester
                Religious Institute in Corporation St, for joint use by
                the Bible Society, the Religious Tract Society and the
                Manchester City Mission (*Manchester Guardian*, 29
                June 1871).
4 Sept.   Dissolution of partnership of Rylands & Cross.
6 Nov.   Mortgage of four Wigan properties, including Gidlow
                House and Buckley House estates, to Edward Byrom
                for £15,000.

1872
3–27 Feb.   John Rylands visited France and Italy with Martha and
                her companion, Miss E.A. Tennant (John Rylands from
                Cannes to W. Linnell, 8 Feb. 1872).
8 June   Death of John Garthwaite Rylands (1826–72) formerly of
                Orrell, at Upholland, last surviving son of John Rylands.
                His will was proved at Liverpool on 21 Aug. 1872.

13 June	Sale of Longford Buildings on Oxford St, Manchester by Thomas Cooke to Reuben Spencer for £44,000.
12 Nov.	Opening of Longford Works in Crewe for the manufacture of ready made clothing on sewing machines (*Crewe Guardian*, 16 Nov. 1872, 8vi.).
28 Nov.	Notice by John Rylands to Reuben Spencer dissolving their partnership. 'The said business has, as from that date (28 Nov. 1872) been carried on, and will henceforth be carried on by the said John Rylands alone on his own account, under the said style or firm of Rylands & Sons'. (*London Gazette*, 14 Nov. 1878, 4994).

1873

5 Feb.	Engagement of Reuben Spencer as Assistant in the business of John Rylands as a Merchant (JRL., Archives of Rylands & Sons Ltd, Index to Deeds & Documents (*c.*1860–1960), 21).
5 Feb.	Grant of power of attorney by John Rylands to Reuben Spencer.
12 May	Notice by John Rylands to Reuben Spencer, determining his engagement as assistant and revoking the grant of power of attorney.
9 July	Lease of land at Gorton for extension of the works.
6 Oct.	Agreement between John Rylands and four of his senior warehousemen, Reuben Spencer, James Horrocks, William Davis Gloyne and William Linnell for the sale of properties valued on 1 July 1873 at £1,024,788 to a company to be called Rylands & Sons Ltd.
25 Oct.	Incorporation of Rylands & Sons Ltd, with a nominal capital of £2,000,000 in £20 shares, nine directors and a governor.
14 Nov.	*The London Gazette* published the notice of dissolution of the partnership of Rylands & Spencer, dated 4 Feb.
18 Dec.	Lease of property in Portland St, Manchester.
22 Dec.	Golden Jubilee of John Rylands (*In memoriam John Rylands*, 1889, 31–3) and endowment of the John Rylands Jubilee Prize at the Manchester Warehousemen and Clerks' Orphan Schools at Cheadle Hulme.

1874

Feb.–March	John Rylands visited France and Italy, staying at Lyons, Cannes, San Remo, Genoa, Florence (John Rylands from Genoa to W. Linnell, 21 Feb. 1874).

16 April	Purchase of Great Bridgewater St Mills for £8,340.
24 April	Lease of offices in Paris, followed by the conclusion of three more Paris leases on 1 May and 15 Oct. 1874 and 6 Feb. 1875.
25 April	Agreement to build a new hall for the Company of Curriers.
7 May	Purchase of Swinton Mills, mortgaged immediately to the vendor James Bowers.
May	Opening of the City Temple for Dr Parker, John Rylands contributing £100 to its building fund (*The British Monthly*, Feb. 1903, 135, 'Dr Joseph Parker').
23 June	Purchase by John Rylands of 1,012 square yards of land with 15 dwelling houses in Burlington St for £1,590. The purchase was probably part of a plan to build a hall of residence adjacent to Owens College for students of the Lancashire Independent College, to whose committee John Rylands had been elected in 1873.
29 July	Lease of a factory in Commercial Rd, London.
10 August	John Rylands first presided over the general meeting of shareholders.
9 Nov.	Purchase of a third site in Liverpool.
17 Nov.	Admission of John Rylands to the freedom of the Company of Curriers.
17 Nov.	Purchase of Waterloo Mills, Chorley, (later renamed the Lancashire Floor Cloth Works) for £9,050 and their immediate mortgage to the vendor.
28 Nov.	Purchase of Hulme St Mills, Manchester, for £64,900.

1875

27 Jan.	Reconveyance by Reuben Spencer of Longford Buildings on payment of mortgage.
13 Feb.	Death of Martha Rylands, aged 69 years, and her interment with Dinah Rylands.
26 June	Purchase by John Rylands of 67 Queen's Gate, Kensington, sited at the junction with Cromwell Rd, from James Shaw for £6,500.
29 June	Purchase of Mather St and Fletcher St Mills, built in Bolton in the 1830s, for £49,277, the bulk of which remained on mortgage loan at three months' notice.
6 Oct.	Marriage of John Rylands of 46 Argyll Rd, Kensington, to Enriqueta Augustina Tennant aged 32 of 54 Palace Gardens Terrace, Kensington, the home of Mrs Leocadia Fernanda Morison (1846–1927), the younger sister of the bride. The ceremony was held in Kensington Congregational Chapel. During the economic depression of 1878–79 John Rylands lent his

new brother-in-law, A.J. Morison, £6,150 against the security of 6 promissory notes dated between 24 Dec. 1878 and 10 April 1879.

23 Dec.   Extension of lease of warehouse in Portland St, Faulkner St and Princess St.

1876

Opening of Abbey Hey School, Gorton, closed in 1894.

Appointment of John Rylands and Reuben Spencer to serve on the Building Committee of the Lancashire Independent College.

Jan.   Last recorded attendance at communion service at Cavendish by John Rylands.

27 Jan.   Lease of part of Compton House, Liverpool.

2 Feb.   John Rylands repaid the mortgage on Longford Hall.

1 May   Lease of mill at Folly Clough, Crawshawbooth.

31 May   John Rylands took the chair at the annual meeting of the Manchester & Salford Asylum for Female Penitents in the Mayor's Parlour of the Town Hall, Manchester. He may have composed the annual report for 1875–76.

29 Dec.   Purchase by John Rylands of four houses called Sunnyside and 2,834 square yards of land on Longford Estate for £1,540.

1877

13 Jan.   Lease of property on London Wall from the Curriers Company.

1 March   Last recorded attendance by John Rylands at a meeting of the firm's board of directors.

14 April   Purchase by John Rylands of land at La Spezia, Italy.

28 June   Purchase by John Rylands of the leasehold interest in the town hall and 1,126 square yards of land from the Stretford Public Hall Co Ltd for £2,100.

22 July   Establishment of a branch in Rio de Janeiro (Index to Deeds & Documents, 23).

27 July   Renewal of lease of Heapey Bleach Works by W.S.C. Standish.

21 Nov.   Establishment of an office in Glasgow.

1878

Jan.   John Rylands and his wife visited the Continent (Mrs E.A. Rylands to W. Linnell, 15 Jan. 1878).

May   John Rylands visited Paris (J. Rylands to W. Linnell, 24 May 1878).

12 May   Lease of land at Horwich for building purposes.

13 Nov.   Lease by Sir Humphrey de Trafford to John Rylands of

Stretford Town Hall and 2,426 square yards for a chief rent of £40 8s.8d.

18 Dec.   Further loan of £10,000 on Wigan properties made by Edward Byrom to John Rylands.

1879

18 Jan.   Mortgage loan of £20,000 made by James Worrall of Ordsall on the security of part of Gorton Mills.

19 June   Purchase by John Rylands of property at 34–37 Via Garibaldi, Rome, valued in 1892 at £6,338.

22 Aug.   Personal guarantee by John Rylands to Hohler & Co. of Cornhill, London, for the payment of bills discounted up to £200,000 in value.

1880

28 Jan.   Lease of a fifth property in Liverpool with warehouse.

3 April   John Rylands visited Paris, in order to cope with the irregular dealings of the firm's local agent, Jules C.A. Fontana, who had been granted power of attorney on 14 Jan. 1879 and who was probably the step-brother of his third wife.

8 April   Award of a knighthood of the Order of the Crown of Italy.

13 May   Ten-year agency agreement concluded with Smith, Youle & Co. for Brazil, which was not renewed upon its expiry by a decision of the directors made on 17 Aug. 1889.

28 May   John Rylands took the chair at the annual meeting of the Manchester & Salford Asylum for Female Penitents, held in the Institute at 99 Embden St, Greenheys.

24 Dec.   Lease of four plots of land in Tib St by John Rylands and Reuben Spencer to the firm.

1881

19 Sept.   Purchase of Corston House, Spencer Rd, Ryde, with 1,300 square yards for £1,600, for use as a rest home for ministers.

12 Nov.   Lease of Gidlow House, Wigan, to Elias Ramicar.

Dec.   Compilation of Catalogue of Longford Hall Library.

1882

4 March   John Rylands subscribed to 1,000 shares, £1 paid, in the Manchester Underwriters Association Ltd.

27 June   John Rylands attended meeting at the residence of Daniel Adamson in Didsbury in order to consider the project of a Manchester Ship Canal.

2 Aug.	Strike by self-actor minders at Gorton Mills (*Gorton Reporter*, 12 Aug. 1882, 8ii; 19 Aug., 8ii).
4 Sept.	John Rylands purchased a £25 share in the Liverpool Cotton Association Ltd. and a £10 share in the Liverpool Cotton Bank Ltd.
11 Oct.	Purchase of Beaulieu House at Haven Street, on the High Road to Ryde with 14.8 acres of land, or about one-third the size of the Longford Estate in Stretford in 1855, for £6,650. The building was renamed Longford House.
20 Oct.	Second mortgage loan of £25,000 made by James Worrall.
8 Dec.	Fire in the Wood St warehouses of the firm in London, causing damages of £300,000.

1883

12 March	Purchase of the Wood St premises for £60,000 from Edward Cheney and Alfred Capel Cure of Badger Hall, Salop. The warehouse block was rebuilt in 1884 in neo-Elizabethan style and had eight storeys but did not adopt sprinklers until 1910.
17 Nov.	John Rylands signed his will.
28 Nov.	The name of John Rylands was removed from the membership roll of Cavendish St Congregational Church.

1884

13 June	Mrs E.A. Rylands bought the Female Penitentiary in Embden St for £1,200.

1885

25 Aug.	John Rylands attended the third meeting of the board of directors of the Manchester Ship Canal Company (Manchester Ship Canal Co., Minutes of the Board of Directors, i, 8, 25 Aug. 1885).

1886

27 July	John Rylands repaid the mortgage of £5,000 on 67 Queen's Gate, Kensington.
31 July	Opening of the Longford Institute at Haven Street, which had been built in 1885 at a total cost of £3,000 after the purchase between 25 May 1883 and 23 June 1884 of five plots of land aggregating 5.35 acres.
1 Sept.	Lease of a plot of land at Haven St in order to build a gasworks for the Institute.
11 Sept.	John Rylands repaid the mortgage of £25,000 on the Wigan properties.

1887

3 Sept.   Mrs Rylands presented a life-sized photograph of John Rylands to the firm for the board room.

29 Sept.   John Rylands recorded his last signature in the Governor's Minute Book.

29 Oct.   John Rylands accepted the post of governor of the University College of North Wales (Minutes of the Board of Directors, i, 44, 29 Oct. 1887).

1888

10 Feb.   John Rylands last presided over a meeting of the company's shareholders.

15 March   John Rylands granted his wife a general power of attorney.

11 Dec.   Death of John Rylands at Longford Hall at the age of 87.

15 Dec.   Ceremony of interment at Southern Cemetery.

16 Dec.   Memorial Services held at Stretford Congregational Church, in the morning by Dr Samuel G. Green and in the evening by the Revd J.W. Kiddle.

1889

1 March   Probate of the will of John Rylands.

30 April   Mrs Rylands acquired a share in the Portico Library.

17 Oct.   Agreement between James Lowe and Mrs Rylands for the sale and purchase of property in Deansgate.

17 Dec.   Conveyance to Mrs Rylands of 1,866 square yards of land in Deansgate for £27,000.

1890

12 March–
23 Sept.   Conclusion of six agreements with the tenants of neighbouring premises in relation to building heights and rights of light.

3 Sept.   Purchase by Mrs Rylands for £1,500 of three more plots of land between Wood St and Spinningfield covering 374 square yards of land.

1892

             Completion of the Rylands Memorial (Fig. 21) in Southern Cemetery.

1893

7 March   Lease by Mrs Rylands to the Stretford Local Board of Stretford Town Hall and the Public Baths together with the library of 3,617 volumes.

16 June   Posthumous grant of arms, comprising a shield, helm and crest, to Mrs Rylands by the College of Arms (Fig. 25).

Figure 24: Memorial Statue of John Rylands, 1894

The original idea of a bust was changed into that of a statue and its location was moved out of the apse so as to occupy a site dominating the nave of the reading room of the library. John Cassidy took immense care over the sculpting of the features. He completed the work in fifteen months and was paid £1,325 or four times the price of £300 for the group of three statues in the foyer, portrayed in Figure 16. C.E. Montague, a senior member of the staff of the *Manchester Guardian*, described the statue as one of a 'philanthropist . . . touched with a spiritual fineness'. *A Hind Let Loose* (Methuen, 1910), 4–5.

(John Rylands Library)

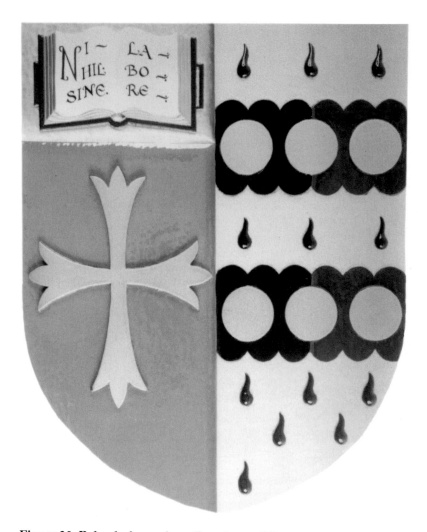

Figure 25: Rylands Arms, impaling those of Tennant, granted in 1893

To the left is portrayed above a cross patonce an open book with the motto chosen by Mrs Rylands and repeated in the crest. To the right the Tennant arms show two bars, each charged with three bezants.

(John Rylands Library)

1894

6 Sept.   Purchase by Mrs Rylands of the chief rent of 67 Queen's Gate for £500 from the earl of Harrington.

11 Dec.   Issue of a certificate of registration of copyright of the armorial bookplate for the John Rylands Library.

28 Dec.   Sale by Mrs Rylands of the Female Penitentiary to the Trustees of the Manchester & Salford Asylum for Female Penitents.

31 Dec.   Repayment by Mrs Rylands of five mortgages taken out on the Market St property of Rylands & Sons Ltd between 1881 and 1891 and totalling £93,106.

1895

13 Jan.   Death of James Horrocks at the age of 62, leaving £70,415 (*Manchester Guardian*, 14 Jan. 1895, 8viii; 15 Jan. 12i).

28 June   Purchase of the Heapey Bleachworks by the firm for £21,000 (JRL., Archives of Rylands & Sons Ltd, Minutes of the Board of Directors, ii, 217, 23 March 1895; 271, 5 July 1895).

1897

8 July   First visit paid to the John Rylands Library by nine American librarians.

5 Nov.   Mrs Rylands bought four flats, 1–4 Avenue Mansions on Finchley Rd, Hampstead for £23,600 and subscribed to 100 shares in the Hampstead Garden Suburb Trust Ltd.

1899

27 Jan.   Purchase by Mrs Rylands of two farms in the eastern Cape for her adopted son Arthur Forbes, who had lived there since 1894. Temple Farm, Cradock, with 1,808 morgen bought for £9,000 and Naauwpoort Farm or 'Longhoek', Steynsburg, with 591 morgen bought for £2,000 guaranteed him a net annual income of £1,000.

25 March   Purchase by Mrs Rylands of Northwood Villa, Buxton, with an estate of 1.1 acres for £8,000.

28 April   J.S. Derbyshire of the Phoenix Fire Office certified that the fireproof premises of the John Rylands Library 'ranked second to none' as 'an exceptional and excellent risk' and were ready for the reception of books, including the Althorp Library.

30 May   The architect Basil Champneys certified that the builders, Morrison & Son, had duly completed work undertaken since Oct. 1897 (JRL., Library Archives, Rylands-Champneys Letters, iv, 109–10).

24 June	Private view of the new Library undertaken by the directors of Rylands & Sons Ltd together with their wives, in the company of Mrs Rylands.
July–Aug.	Large-scale transfer of books from Longford Hall (JRL., Library Archives, E.G. Duff to Mrs Rylands, 23 Aug. 1899).
6 Oct.	Inauguration of the John Rylands Library.
14 Oct.	Inauguration of the John Rylands Wing at the Manchester Warehousemen and Clerks' Orphan Schools, Cheadle Hulme.
4 Dec.	Incorporation of Rylands & Sons (Africa) Ltd, with a capital of £10,000, renamed in 1900 Rylands & Sons (Colonial) Ltd.

1900

1 Feb.	Conveyance of the new Library to the Trustees of the John Rylands Library.
June	Insurance of the books for £200,000.
Sept.	Insurance of the building for £70,000.

1901

22 May	Death of Reuben Spencer at the age of 70, leaving £201,106.

1905

23 June	Purchase by Mrs Rylands of Fairholme Villa on Lincombe Hill, Torquay with an estate of 1,815 square yards for £10,000.
21 Sept.	Purchase by Mrs Rylands of 'Cyprus', on Ridgway Rd, Torquay, for £750.

1906

31 Oct.	Purchase of 250–258 Deansgate with 640 square yards for £10,250.
6 Nov.	Purchase of 244–246 Deansgate for £4,500, the two acquisitions providing the site for the Congregational Church House opened in 1911.

1907

15 July	Purchase of the Cheshire Cheese Hotel in Wood St with 476 square yards for £7,150 in order to provide space for the future extension of the John Rylands Library.

1908

4 Feb.	Death of Enriqueta Augustina Rylands.

1909
23 April   Death of Hilda Flemmer (1881–1909), at Middelburg, Cape Colony. Hilda had marrried Arthur Forbes after concluding an ante-nuptial contract on 15 April 1902.

1919
8 Oct.   Death of William Carnelley at the age of 96, leaving £358,864.

1930
4 Feb.   N.R.D. Tennant paid Manchester Corporation £340 for the care and upkeep of the Rylands Memorial in Southern Cemetery.

1937
17 Aug.   Final Release of the estate of Mrs E.A. Rylands, after the supplementary releases of 25 July 1912 and 10 March 1925.

1952

Listing of the John Rylands Library as a building of regional importance with two star status (Grade II★), a ranking confirmed in 1974 and in 1993.

1972
19 July   Merger of the John Rylands Library and the Library of the University of Manchester.

15. *Bibliography*

Unpublished sources

Companies House, Department of Trade and Industry, Cardiff, and the Public Record Office, Kew
   Company File of Rylands & Sons Ltd, 1873–1989, No. 7748.

Greater Manchester Record Office
   Archives of the Manchester Ship Canal Company, Minutes of the Board of Directors, 1885–88.

John Rylands Library, Manchester

1.   Carnelley Manuscripts, two boxes containing 21 items relating to William Carnelley (1823–1919) and donated in 1984 by his grand-daughter, Miss E. Austin.

2.   English Manuscript 1140, catalogued in 1950, being the Catalogue of the Library of John Rylands at Longford Hall, 1881, 2 vols.

3.   English Manuscript 1185 in two volumes presented in 1956 by Messrs Dendy, Patterson and Simpsons of Manchester. These volumes seem to have been the personal business files of John Rylands and contain extensive entries in his own handwriting.

4.   Archives of Rylands & Sons Ltd, donated by Family Hampers Ltd, of Leeds in 1984 through the agency of the Business Archives Council.

5.   Rylands Papers presented by Mr L.H. Orford in 1968 and including the surviving personal papers of Enriqueta A. Rylands. This collection includes the wills of John Rylands and of Enriqueta Augustina Rylands.

Manchester Central Library, Archives Department
   Archives of Cavendish Street Congregational Church, listed at M162.
   Chapman Manuscripts, listed at M95, including deeds relating to the lease, mortgage and purchase of Gorton Mills (1841–73).

Registry of Births, Marriages and Deaths, London and Trafford.
   Death Certificates of John Rylands, his three wives and his son William Rylands.

Wigan Record Office, Leigh
    Deeds of Joseph Rylands (1767–1847), father of John Rylands,
    two boxes numbered D/DX/E1/127, 128.

John Linnell, Esq., of Poynton, Cheshire
    The Linnell Papers preserved by Ruth Linnell (1906–89) and
    including letters of John Rylands from 1872 and of Enriqueta
    Rylands from 1878.

D.A. Farnie, 'John Rylands of Longford Hall: a comment upon the
    Report by Mr J. Ayers with particular reference to the three
    pages (pp.6–9) relating to John Rylands', a 24-page manuscript
    dated 29 June 1992 and prepared in response to the relevant
    part of a consultant's report dated 26 March 1992, entitled
    'The architectural and historical interest of Longford Hall' and
    submitted to Trafford Borough Council.

Printed sources

Ashton, T.S., 'Rylands & Sons Ltd (1823)', *Manchester Guardian
    Commercial,* 5 May 1934, 9.
Barker, N., *Bibliotheca Lindesiana* (Quaritch, 1978)
Binfield, J.C.G., *So down to prayers: studies in English nonconformity,
    1780–1920* (Dent, 1977).
Boase, F., *Modern English Biography* (Truro: Netherton, 1901; Cass,
    1965), iii, 368.
Bourne, H.R. Fox, *The romance of trade* (Cassell, 1876), 219–23.
British Trade Journal, 1 April 1887, 277–8, 'British Industries. No
    CLXXVII – Messrs Rylands & Sons (Limited), Manchester,
    London, & c'.
The century's progress: Lancashire (London Printing and Engraving
    Company, 1892), 73–4.
Commerce, 5 July 1893, 17–23, Lesser Columbus (Lawrence
    Cowen), 'A Lancashire lesson'.
Crofton, H.T., *A history of the ancient chapel of Stretford in Manchester
    parish* (Manchester: Chetham Society, 1903), iii, 164–6.
Deiss, E., *À travers l'Angleterre industrielle et commerciale (notes de
    voyage)* (Paris: Guillaumin, 1898), 175–83.
The Draper, Supplement to, 28 March 1903, 18–19, 'Rylands & Sons
    Ltd, manufacturers and merchants'.
Edwards, John, 'John Rylands', *Y Traethodydd* (Caernarfon, Davies,
    May 1891), 47:cxc, 184–94.
Farnie, D.A., 'Enriqueta Augustina Rylands (1843–1908), founder
    of the John Rylands Library', *Bulletin of the John Rylands
    University Library of Manchester,* 71:2 (Summer 1989), 3–38.
Farnie, D.A. *The English cotton industry and the world market
    1815–1896* (Oxford: Clarendon Press, 1979).

Farnie, D.A. 'John Rylands (1801–88)' in D.J. Jeremy (ed.), *Dictionary of business biography* (Butterworth, 1985), 4, 999–1004.

Farnie, D.A. 'John Rylands of Manchester', *Bulletin of the John Rylands Library of the University of Manchester*, 56:2 (Autumn 1973), 93–129.

Farnie, D.A. 'The structure of the British cotton industry, 1846–1914' in Akio Okochi and Shin-ichi Yonekawa (eds), *The textile industry and its business climate: proceedings of the Fuji conference* (Tokyo: University Press, 1982, International Conference on Business History), viii, 45–91.

Farnie, D.A. & Shin-ichi Yonekawa, 'The emergence of the large firm in the cotton spinning industries of the world, 1883–1938', *Textile History*, 19:2 (Autumn 1988), 171–210.

Fortunes made in business: life struggles of successful people (Amalgamated Press, 1901), 9–17, 'A cotton prince'.

[Green, S.G.], *In memoriam John Rylands born February 7, 1801, died December 11, 1888* (Chilworth: Unwin, 1889, 72pp., printed on behalf of Mrs Rylands for private circulation). The author is identified as Dr Green by C.W. Sutton in the article cited below. He quotes from the diary of John Rylands (21, 55).

Green, S.G. 'The John Rylands Library', *The Leisure Hour*, Dec. 1899, 138–45.

Green, S.G., 'The late Mr John Rylands of Manchester', *Sunday At Home*, 23 March 1889, 181–6.

Higson, J., *The Gorton historical recorder* (Droylsden: Higson, 1852), 171–208.

Kazuhiko Kondo, 'John Rylands and *The protestant ethic and The spirit of capitalism*' [in Japanese], *Shiso* [Thought], 714 (1983), 24–43.

Manchester & Salford Asylum for Female Penitents, Annual Reports, 1823–80.

Manchester City News, 1 April 1865, 2vi, 3i–ii; 8 April, 2vi–vii, 3i; 15 April, 2v–vii, 3i–ii, 'Principal Manchester firms – their rise and progress'. No. V. Messrs. Rylands & Sons', largely written by or with the help of Reuben Spencer.

Manchester of today (Historical Publishing Company, 1888), 79–81.

Parker, J. 'The story of the cotton king: recollections of John Rylands, of Manchester', *The Young Man: a Monthly Journal and Review*, April 1893, 111–14, reprinted in the *Manchester City News*, 1 April 1893, 2iv–v, 'Dr Parker's recollections of John Rylands' and in the *Daily News*, 7 October 1899, 8i–iii, J. Parker, 'John Rylands of Manchester', reprinted from *A preacher's life* (Hodder, 1899), 142–58. The writer was a Congregationalist divine whose ministry in Manchester lasted for eleven years from 1858 to 1869. The depth of his insight into the character of Rylands is rivalled only by that of Dr Green.

Pike, G.H., *Dr Parker and his friends* (Unwin, 1904), 48–64, 'John Rylands of Manchester'.

Rubinstein, W.D., 'British millionaires, 1809–1949', *Bulletin of the Institute of Historical Research*, 47 (1974), 202–23.

Rubinstein, W.D., *Men of property: the very wealthy in Britain since the industrial revolution* (Croom Helm, 1981).

Shaw, W.A., *Manchester old and new* (Cassell, 1894), ii, 35–8.

Simpson, A.W.B., 'Legal liability for bursting reservoirs: the historical context of *Rylands v. Fletcher*', *Journal of Legal Studies*, 13:2 (1984), 209–64.

Spencer, R., *The home trade of Manchester with personal reminiscences and occasional notes* (Simpkin, 1890), 145–61.

Sutton, C.W., 'John Rylands (1801–88)' in the *Dictionary of national biography*, xviii, (1897), 548–9, supplemented by the material used by the author and contained in the collection of newspaper cuttings – biography, s.v. Rylands, John in the Local Studies Library of the Manchester Central Library.

Thompson, F.M.L., 'Life after death: how successful nineteenth-century businessmen disposed of their fortunes', *Economic History Review*, second series, 43 (1990), 40–61.

Tracy, W.B. and W.J. Pike, *Manchester and Salford at the close of the nineteenth century: contemporary biographies* (Brighton: Pike, 1899), 265.